To rain
3 viv

455 7877 S Mclane Ste
Buchner

Marianne Gill
Marriott 541-301-0690

excuse me, your *life* is waiting

excuse me, your *life* is waiting

the astonishing power of feelings

lynn grabhorn

Beyond Books
9221 58th Ave. S.E.
Olympia, WA. 98513
888-509-0200

ISBN: 0-9673067-0-1

Library of Congress Catalog Card Number 98-075449
Grabhorn, Lynn
Excuse Me, Your LIFE Is Waiting

Jacket design: Douglas Oliver Design Office, Santa Monica, CA 90404
Cover illustration: Craig Fraizer, Mill Valley, CA 94941
Copyediting: Vicki McCown, Anacortes, WA 98221
Test design and layout: Turner Type & Design, Lacey, WA 98503
Photograph: Ed Fitzgerald, Lacey, WA 98503

Manufactured in the United States of America
10 9 8 7 6 5 4 3 2

Dedication

To every one of us
who finally...maybe...possibly...
believes they have
the right to perpetual happiness,
beginning now.

CONTENTS

Introduction

For well over a decade my passion has been a grand spiritual journey into what I call "the physics of thought," toward the end that a deeper knowledge of this somewhat outrageous topic might provide ways for all of us—myself in particular—to get more out of life.

My studies have taken me everywhere from learned professors of physics to deep within the esoteric sciences, from plain old medicine and just about everything in between to the point where I decided I could call myself somewhat of a lay expert on the subject. The only problem was that, knowledge or no, "getting more out of life" wasn't happening and it was beginning to tick me off. Something was missing, and I flat-out couldn't put my finger on it.

Naturally, with my vast knowledge on the subject, when I came across some new but provincial teachings from this unlettered, unscientific family of teachers, my first impulse was to pooh-pooh the information because of their enormous oversimplification of what I considered to be a rather formidable topic. So it was more than a tad begrudgingly that I agreed to investigate this taped malarkey that a well-meaning friend had ungraciously shoved in my face.

I flipped! Here I am, this learned student of thought —its magnetics, its propellant, its frequencies, its relation to emotion, its effect on our experience, etc.—and these guys come along to nonchalantly provide, in the simplest of form, the missing pieces to life's obstacles that I was beginning to think didn't exist. Sort of like, "Aaa, pardon me, ma'am, might this be what you were looking for?"

So I dive into this information (ultimately hundreds of hours worth) and in two weeks I'm stunned, in one month I'm flabbergasted, and in ninety days there's such a turn around in my life, I say, "That's it! I gotta write about it so the rest of the world can flip along with me."

Now I grant you, there are probably eight and a half million books on the over-worked subject of getting more out of life, but the utterly bizarre thing about these little-known principles are (a) they are uncomplicated, (b) they work fast, and, (c) they are guaranteed.

And so, in my own prosaic words and style I've reissued here the profoundly simple teachings from the Hicks family in Texas,* spiced with my own angles and buzzwords, my own observations and experiences over the past years, and blended it together with my years of study. I unashamedly offer the finished product as the greatest missing link to life and living ever known to mankind, which means I've done this stuff...am still doing it...and will never stop doing it...because, by damn, it works!

lynn grabhorn

*PO Box 690070, San Antonio, TX 78269

how we got in this mess

How do we get what we get in life? Why do some people seem to have it all while others suffer so? Why did that bozo bump into you on the freeway? Why did that little child have to die so young? How come that guy got promoted, and not you? Why can't everybody have prosperity, and joy, and security?

In our everlasting search to find more happiness in life, we devour positive-thinking books by the millions. But if those books truly hold the secrets to an abundant and joyful life, why do we keep buying new ones? Oh sure, there are a few that have come close to giving us the keys to that elusive "good life," but no true winners; our lives don't do a lot of changing. "Maybe it was just the wrong book," we rationalize. "Let's try another one." Or another religion. Or a different kind of meditation. Or another teacher, or psychic, or doctor, or relationship.

We reach out anywhere and everywhere for relief from the tedium and struggle of daily living, yet the vast majority of us are still looking. How come? How come we've never learned the simple secret to living the good life, whatever that may represent to us? How come we continue to whack and scratch like frantic mad dogs to get what we want, when all along the key to obtaining our innermost desires has been as elemental as life itself?

If you really think that things come to you by some stroke of good or bad luck, or by accident, or coincidence, or by knocking your brains out against some very unsympathetic stone walls, then get a grip. This book could be dangerous to your discontent.

Slugger Jessie

Years ago, long before I had ever heard about the Law of Attraction, my friend Mindy insisted I go with her to see a Little League game. Her son played left field, but that's not why she wanted me to go with her.

The size of the weekend crowd surprised me. You'd have thought Babe Ruth himself was reincarnating for a guest appearance. But question her as I might, no amount of prodding would cut loose Mindy's little intrigue. So what the heck; I went along with it.

Her son came up to bat and struck out. Our side got two hits but no runs before the side was retired. Then came the other guys; you couldn't help but feel the crowd's excitement. A couple of young bull dogs strolled to the plate and promptly struck out, thanks to our team's terrific pitcher. Now it was Jessie's turn, and the cheers began. From both sides.

Jessie was small, I mean really small. His bat seemed longer than he was. He stepped up to the plate with unceremonious confidence and proceeded to hit the very first ball so far out over the bushes that they never did find it. I was flabbergasted, the crowd went ballistic, and Mindy looked at me and winked.

This impossible scenario repeated itself four more times. Little Slugger Jessie was a sensation, a phenomenon in the flesh. And with the research I was doing on the physics of manifesting, I damn sure wanted to find out what made this little half-pint tick, just as Mindy knew I would.

When most of the back-slapping was over, I wedged my way up to him through the crowd and asked if we could sit down and talk for a minute. When we reached the top of the bleachers I said, "Jessie, how do you do that? How do you hit so many home runs?"

"I dunno," he offered innocently, waving a casual goodbye to some of his teammates. "Each time I get up to bat I just feel what it's gonna be like to connect, and I do."

Although I didn't know it at the time, Jessie had just described the fundamental principle of manifestation known as the Law of Attraction, the physics that creates every moment of our day.

Today Jess lives in style with a lovely wife, two great kids, a house of collectibles from their worldly travels, and a computer from which he makes copious amounts of dollars managing his investments. He passed over baseball as a career because he wanted to be his own boss on his own time. How has he become so successful? Same way he hit the ball: by feeling. Not by thought alone, by *feeeeeling!*

"Human Condition," My Foot

Didn't it ever strike you as bizarre that our lives should be so tough when we're all so brilliant? Here we are, this hugely intelligent species that can split atoms, fly to the moon and create the Flintstones, yet we're all running around blowing each other up, having heart attacks or starving to death. It makes no sense. How did we get into this mess? Or is it just the so-called human condition?

It all began uncountable eons ago with the first untrue declarations from those who desired power which proclaimed that our lives revolved around, and were the result of, circumstances over which we had no control, including being dominated by others. Since that's what everybody has believed for untold eons, that's what we still believe to this day.

And so, like our parents before us and theirs before them, all the way back for God knows how many thousands of years, we have struggled, whacked, strained, worried, and died long before our time from the all too unnecessary demands of living. We believed it to be the human condition, part of the unfortunate affliction we have come to call reality.

But the human condition is a myth. And so, for that matter, is what we call reality.

The truth is, in our everyday natural state, we have the sacred ability to maneuver this thing called "our life" to be any way we want it to be. *Any way!* Bar nothing! From a happy family to a filled-in ozone layer.

So why haven't the zillions of books written on how to have it all, how to think and get rich, how to visualize our way to success, and how to acquire power through positive thinking shown us how to help ourselves out of this mess? Simple! Every one of those books left out the most important key of all time to life and living:

We create by feeling, not by thought!

That's right, we get what we get by the way we feel, not by trying to slug things into place or control our minds. Every car accident, job promotion, great or lousy lover, full or empty bank account comes to us by the most elemental law of physics: like attracts like. And since most of us haven't felt too hot about what we've had for most of our lives, we've become highly gifted masters at attracting an overabundance of circumstances we'd rather not have.

You want a new car? You got it! You want to work successfully for yourself? You got it! You want to close that deal? Make more money? Have a great relationship? Live without fear? Have a spiritually fulfilling life? Have superb health, freedom, independence? You got it, *if* you know how to *feeeeel* it into being.

The Law of Attraction—like attracts like—is absolute (and has nothing to do with personalities). No one lives beyond this law, for it is the law of the universe. It's just that we never realized until recently that the law applies to us too. This is the law behind success or failure. It's what causes fender-benders or fatalities. It is, to the point, what runs every waking moment of our lives.

So if we want to turn our lives around, or bring in greater abundance, or health, or safety, or happiness of any kind, we have only to learn the simple steps of manipulating our "feelings", and a whole new world of plenty opens for the asking.

We Were Taught Backwards

Most of us haven't a clue how we get what we get in life. First there's that long list of things we want and never get, nor ever hope to get. Then there's that even longer list of all the things we don't want, yet seem to get more of with disheartening regularity. No one's to blame for this ceaseless dreambusting. We were just taught backwards.

Probably the most destructive thing we've been taught is that life is born of a series of circumstances served up to us on this gigantic platter called Pot Luck, or Fate, starting always with the parents we were born to and the environment in which we grew up. If we were born rich, we got a lucky draw. If we were born poor, struggle would be our more common destiny. If we found happiness, it was by the cherished touch of Lady Luck. If some drunken idiot crashed into us on the freeway, it was rotten fate.

We've been taught that we gain only as we labor, that action is the magic word. Do, do, do; work, work, work, strive, sweat, toil, and then if our luck holds, we just might come out ahead.

We've been taught by loving, misguided elders to be cautious and guarded. "Don't climb the tree, honey, or you'll fall." "Don't wear that silly thing, or people will laugh." "Don't forget to lock your doors, or you'll be robbed." We've become such a defensive species, our entire lives revolve around fearful credos of Be Careful, Be Cautious, Be Safe and Secure. Heaven forbid we should ever let that guard down!

But the greatest obstacle to living our potential comes from toddler days when we were trained to look for what's wrong—with everything! With our jobs, our cars, our relationships, our clothes, our shapes, our health, our freeways, our planet, our faith, our entertainment, our children, our government, even our friends. Yet most of the world can't even agree about what right or wrong is, so we war, and strike, and demonstrate, and make laws, and go to psychiatrists.

"That's life," you say. "We have to take the good with the bad, the ups with the downs. We have to be on guard, work hard, do things right, be watchful and hope for a break. Yes, that's the way life is."

No, no, and NO! That is simply not the way real Life is, and it's time we faced up to how we actually do create what we have in our world, our empty or full bank accounts, our grand or boring jobs, our good fortune or bad, and everything else in this arena we so nonchalantly call reality.

How do we do it? Don't laugh; it all comes from...*how we're vibrating!*

Look, Ma, I'm Vibrating

Everything in this world is made of energy: you, me, the rock, the table, the blades of grass. And since energy is actually vibration, that means that everything that exists vibrates. Everything! Including you and me.

Modern-day physicists have finally come to agree that energy and matter are one and the same, which brings us back to where we started: that everything vibrates, because everything—whether you can see it or not—is energy. Pure, pulsing, ever-flowing energy.

But even though there's only one energy, it vibrates differently. Just like the sound that pours out of a musical instrument, some energy vibrates fast (such as high notes) from high frequencies, and some vibrates slow (such as low notes) from low frequencies. Unlike the tones from a musical instrument, however, the energy that flows out from us comes from our highly charged emotions to create highly charged *electromagnetic* wave patterns of energy, making us powerful—but volatile—walking magnets.

That's nice, but who cares? Well, if you want to know why you've had to struggle so hard with your life, you do! If you want to know how to change your life to be exactly the way you want it to be, you had darn well better care, because the electromagnetic vibrations you send out every split second of every day are what have brought—and are continuing to bring—everything into your life, big or small, good or bad. Everything! *No exceptions.*

From No Commissions to No Commissions

Central California is a mecca for those who love to sell land. Cattle ranches, vineyards, resorts, residential developments, dairy farms, planned communities; if you have the know-how and patience to bring a deal to the table where all parties are panting to sign, you can make a fortune from the gargantuan commissions.

Tom was an acquaintance of mine who did just that with outrageous regularity. He was a real estate broker in his mid-forty's (we were about the same age), and an acknowledged pro with commercial land sales.

I had just sold another business in Los Angeles and moved to the central coast with no idea of what to do next, until I met Tom. Within a few months I acquired my real estate license and began my apprenticeship in earnest under Tom's masterful tutelage in his well-known real estate office. Since my sales would fatten his pocket as well as mine, he took the time to teach me well. We'd spend long hours poring over comparisons of grape harvests, soil tests, and potential feed yields of various land segments that would be capable of sustaining "X" number of cattle. Considering the closest I had ever been to a cow or cattle was store-bought milk and steak, and that while I had once been a hearty drinker, what I knew about wines would fit on a pinhead, I found the instruction fascinating.

Tom worked with me for months before allowing me to get my feet wet. While I was learning about this new world, I was also developing a plan to market central California lands to off-shore buyers. By the time I had finished the first phase of my apprenticeship, I had formed the specialized real estate firm of Western Lands, USA, along with a marketing concept that was so flawless, I wondered why no one else had thought of it before me.

That's where I made my first mistake. My plan was so easy, so fool-proof, so ready and ripe to produce huge sales, I just knew there had to be something wrong with it. It was too good. It would all happen too fast. Someone would steal it. In fact it was so good, it flat-out spooked me.

Finally the day came. I was out showing my first chunk of land, a large ranch overlooking the magnificent coastline of Big Sur, California. Not only was the price well into the millions, but the commission would be far more than I had made collectively during my entire working life. In a few weeks, buyer and seller agreed. I had a sale and went into instant panic.

Tom was pleased; everybody was pleased; I was terrified. And the closer we got to closing, the more paranoid I became. It was all too good to be true, too easy, too incredible. My stomach churned like a packed washing machine.

Tom pooh-poohed my fears by telling me how proud he was of me, and that he had never seen such a clean, uncomplicated deal. But I was a nervous wreck. It was too unreal, it would never happen. And it didn't! On the day—the *day*—the big sale was to close, the buyer found legal cause to back out. My worst fears had come to pass.

Twice more that happened until I finally told Tom I just couldn't handle the pressure and stress of these big-commission closings that came down to the wire but never happened. All he ever said was, "Sweetie, you blew 'em away with your fears. You gotta feel those tender little suckers close, feel yourself shaking everybody's hand, and feel yourself out there celebrating. You gotta know it's going to work, honey, or trust me, it never will. If you can't feel it happening, it won't."

I didn't have a clue what he was talking about. After the first sale bombed, I had immersed myself in all the best-selling books on positive thinking and how to get rich quick. But when two more sales blew up in my face that were also within days and hours of closing, I decided this potential fantasyland was not for me, and opted to open a mortgage company which had considerably less apprehension involved.

It wasn't until years later when I had finally gotten involved with the Law of Attraction that I realized what Tom meant. Without even realizing what he was doing, Tom had learned to command energy to his advantage. Instinctively he knew that closing deals meant more than just thinking big, thinking positive, or making good contracts. Tom, like Jessie, somehow knew you had to *feel* your desires into being.

Tuning Forks and the Law of Attraction

Way back in the thirties a couple of guys in the Orient were attempting to prove that thoughts were real things, and that different kinds of thoughts create different kinds of vibrations. So they decided to see if they could actually photograph vibrations of thought. And by golly they did, right through steel walls, an experiment that's been replicated many times since.

But they also proved something else perhaps even more important. They found that the more emotion

11

the thinker/sender charged his thoughts with, the clearer the picture turned out to be! These fellows were possibly the first to prove that there is magnetic energy attached to our thoughts, and that thought is propelled by our emotions. What they missed, though, is that because the vibrational waves (emotions) we send out are magnetically charged, we are literally walking magnets, constantly pulling back into our world anything that just happens to be playing on the same frequency or wavelength.

For instance, when we're feeling up, filled with joy and gratitude, our emotions are sending out high frequency vibrations that will magnetize only good stuff back to us, meaning anything with the same high vibratory frequency that matches what we're sending out. Like attracts like.

On the other hand, when we're experiencing anything that joy *isn't,* such as fear, worry, guilt, or even mild concern, those emotions are sending out low-frequency vibrations. Since low frequencies are every bit as magnetic as high frequencies, they're going to attract only cruddy stuff back to us, meaning anything of that same low frequency that will cause us to feel (and vibrate) as lousy as what we're sending out. Cruddy out, cruddy back; it's always a vibrational match.

So whether it's high vibrational joy, or low vibrational worry, what we're vibrationally offering in any moment is what we're attracting back. We are the initiators of the vibrations, therefore the magnets, the cause. Like it or not, we have created—and are creating—it all. We may be flesh and blood, but first and foremost we are energy—

magnetic energy at that! Which makes us living, breathing magnets. (Don't you love it? You may *think* you're president of a Fortune 500 company, or a mother and wife, or valedictorian of your class, or an airline mechanic, but what you really are is a walking magnet! Ah, little did you know.)

Crazy as that may sound, it's high time we woke up to the fact that we are electromagnetic beings tripping around with this mindboggling capacity to magnetize into our lives whatever in the world we desire by controlling the *feelings* that come from our thoughts.

But because we exist on this planet in a predominantly low frequency field of energy born of eight billion people who are vibrating more feelings of stress and fearfulness than joy, we involuntarily take in those vibrations and react to them. Which means that until we consciously learn to override the pervasive low frequencies in which we exist, we will keep recycling unpleasant outcomes into our lives day after tiresome day. Just like swimming in salt water, if we don't wash the residue off, sooner or later it's going to make us mighty uncomfortable.

There's just no way around it; the way we feel is the way we attract. And more often than not those feelings come from our thoughts, setting up the instantaneous electromagnetic chain reactions that ultimately cause things to happen, to be created, to be withheld, or to be destroyed (like my big commissions).

So, once again: Our feelings go out from us in electromagnetic waves. Whatever frequency goes out will automatically attract its identical frequency, thus causing things to happen—good or bad—by finding their matching vibrations.

Happy, high vibrations attract happy, high vibrational circumstances. Yucky, low vibrations attract yucky low vibrational circumstances. In both cases, what comes back causes us to feel just as high or low as what we had been transmitting (feeling), because it's an exact vibrational match to what we sent out.

It's the same principle as a tuning fork. Ding a tuning fork in a room filled with all different kinds of tuning forks calibrated to various pitches, and only the ones calibrated to the *same frequency* as the one you just dinged will ding too, even if they're way across the Astrodome. Like forces attract; it's a classic rule of physics.

But unlike a tuning fork which never changes its tonal frequency, we humans with our ever-changing emotions flip-flop our frequencies and magnetic intensities all over the place like lotto balls in a blow machine. One minute we can be as high as a kite and as powerful as the sun, and, in the very next, about as turned-on energetically as a cardboard box under the couch. What flips us around like that comes from the kinds of—and intensity of—*feeeeelings* we're having: from luke warm happy to way up, or from just blah to way down.

So instead of being one, constant, well-aimed tuning fork, we're more like a whole bunch of them clustered together, each having a different pitch or frequency, and collectively pinging haphazardly all over the place with our up-down, up-down emotions. Since one minute we're pinging high and the next minute we're pinging low, causing one frequency to cancel out the other, nothing much ever changes in our lives, or at least not very rapidly.

Only we're not tuning forks. What's coming back to us as a result of the jumble of unfocused emotional energy (vibrations) we spew out every instant are rarely pleasant little pings, but a relentless procession of messed-up, hit or miss, unplanned events and circumstances.

Needless to say, what we've been creating with all this indiscriminate flowing of energy is pure pandemonium at worst and a second-rate life at best as we continue magnetizing into our day-to-day existence every experience, person, game, happening, encounter, incident, event, hazard, occasion, or episode *by however we happen to be vibrating*. Which means feeling.

Bills, Bills, Bills

Take a not-too favorite topic for example: paying bills. Unless you're in super financial shape, how do you usually feel when it gets to be bill-paying time? Thrilled? Elated? Euphoric? Not likely. How about worried, anxious, or plain old down? Join the group!

Well, here's the kicker: it's due to those very feelings of despair that we keep on having such a hard time with the bills! Why? *Because whatever we're feeling is what we're vibrating, and whatever we're vibrating is what we're attracting.* Universal law. That's just the way it is.

Tony and his wife, Ginger, and I got together regularly to compare notes about our progress with the Law of

Attraction. Thank heavens they were around, since they were the only folks I knew who lived close by where I could let my hair down and compare notes.

One night as we were finishing dinner at my place, we began reminiscing over how it used to be in those times before we got involved in controlling energy. The conversation was light and comical until Tony started talking about how ugly it had been trying to pay bills with no money. While I always enjoyed their company, the feelings that began to surface from this conversation were making me uncomfortable, as I had only recently started to come out of a long and difficult financial drought. I wanted the conversation to change. It didn't.

Tony had always made a decent living, and with their kids grown and gone, the two of them could have gotten along easily on his income alone. But Ginger wanted to stretch her work-wings again, so she went back into the real estate business she had left years ago. This was well before Law of Attraction years, but nonetheless, she did quite well. "Why was it, then," they reminisced as I was pouring coffee, "that we'd never have enough money to pay our bills?"

"I presume you just overextended yourselves whenever Ginger made a hit," I said, hoping to ward off the emotional discourse I knew was coming about how tough it was to live without enough money in the bank.

"Sure we did," laughed Tony. "We were living it up until we realized what a mess we had gotten ourselves into. We had already refinanced the house, so that wasn't an option. We had never saved much of anything, so we had no reserves to fall back on. And now here we were with all this new income coming in, but somehow worse off than we were before, with more bills we couldn't pay. If Ginger had a good closing, we were almost okay. But if nothing was moving for her, we were in deep trouble and it would take us months to recover."

"Uh huh, I know the feeling. But isn't it great how that's all behind us now?" I tried to leap-frog the conversation into a new direction, but Ginger was having none of it. For whatever reason, she needed to relive those painful days.

"I swear," Ginger went on, "it got so bad every month, that when it came time to pay those fool things—which I put off for as long as I could—I'd either break out in a rash or have a migraine. I'd pull out the stack, put it on the desk, and just look at it for a day or two. Then I'd get that horrible sinking feeling in the pit of my stomach because I knew that what we had to pay and what we had in the bank simply didn't match. So I'd pick out one bill and decide how much I could get away with paying. It was awful. You know what that was like, Lynn; you've been there."

"More times than I care to count," I reflected.

"Thank heavens that's all changed," sighed Tony, looking fondly at Ginger. "Another year of that and you'd be collecting on my life insurance." As he reached across the table for Ginger's hand, my heart warmed as I saw her eyes tear up with the happiness they both were experiencing now. They had turned their financial corner a couple of years ago, transforming their lives into abundance and sublime happiness. They had learned how to command energy. What contentment vibrated between them. And what a long way they'd come. What a long way we all had come!

Tony and Ginger and I had spent years in various degrees of financial chaos because we didn't know a thing about controlling our energy. Each in our own way, as bill-paying time came and we'd look at how much we needed but didn't have, the more uptight we'd get. The more we focused on what we didn't have, the greater our negative energies would grow, magnetizing even more debt along with less income to offset it.

Our emotional focus on the lack of what we had was continuing to magnetize more of the same back into our experience, usually bigger and meaner and nastier than the month before.

The process is like tossing a boomerang, one of those things you pitch away from you that circles back for you to catch (or clobber you if you're not looking). What we send out—vibrationally—is what we get back. So until we change our vibrations, we're going to pull back to us whatever we've sent out.

To put it another way, if we don't stop feeling—and sending out—downer vibrations, then downer circumstances are all we're going to pull back!

We get what we emotionally focus on! Focus on what we want with passion and excitement, and presto! It's on its way. Focus on what we don't want with the same passion (such as worry, concern, etc.) and presto! It too will be on its way.

The universe doesn't give a crapshoot whether we want something or don't want something; it works strictly off of the physics principle we call the Law of Attraction. We send the magnetic feelings out, the universe obediently delivers. It doesn't react to our pleas; it only responds to our vibrations which come purely from how we're feeling.

Does it matter what caused the feelings in the first place? No. They could come from a thought, from an outside event, or just from a general mood. But regardless of how they are initiated, the events that make up our lives come solely from our moment-to-moment, day-to-day, year-to-year outflow of feelings.

Focus, Get Bigger

So let's get real here for a minute. No one is suggesting we walk around being goody-two-shoes all day long, trying to be happy about just being fired or missing the train or misplacing our car keys.

But facts are facts. Since what we send out is what we get back, and since what we send out comes from what we've been focusing on, it might behoove us to pay a damn sight more attention to what we're thinking about, *and how that is making us feeeeel.*

Focus on what we want, and it will come if we don't sabotage it. Focus on what we don't want, and it comes too, usually with more of a wallop to it than it had to begin with!

Back to the bills. Let's say you've been having a whole batch of thoughts about how much you don't like paying them. Each one of those thoughts (which is very much alive) carries the emotional vibration, or signature, from when you thought it, and it goes out to find and hook up with other thoughts that have identical vibrations. When two thoughts of the same emotional intensity come together, they vibrate more powerfully at a higher, faster frequency then one by itself.

So now, instead of just one little old insignificant thought out there about your bills, you've got a bigger and more powerful one than you had to begin with, because every time you think about it, it joins up and clumps together with the ones you sent out before. Ah, but there's more.

You not only have your *own* downer thoughts about bills clumping together out there and growing bigger and more powerful with each new dejected feeling you send out, but now they're joining up with other downer thought-balls on the same frequency sent out from other people. About anything. I call them junk bombs. They clump together in matching frequencies of fear and anxiety, and can easily be headed back your way unless you get yourself turned around emotionally. Meaning that sooner or later, one or more of those junk bombs with all sorts of unpleasant stuff attached to it from everybody else's worries is going to come back and sock you loud and hard *IF* you're still vibrating the same way and broadcasting your wavelength on the same frequency.

Now you have a real mess on your hands; more bills than you had in the first place, along with a lot more disagreeable circumstances that may or may not have to do with paying those bills. Your car breaks down, and you don't have the dollars to fix it. Your washer goes on the fritz. Your kids break someone's window. Your dog attacks some nice soul out for a walk. And on Super

Bowl Sunday, with a houseful of rabid fans, your TV blows its stack.

Your "attracting magnet" is powerfully turned on with that emotionally charged downer vibration, and will keep on attracting more garbage like a homing beacon until you change that vibration. Once you do, the boomerang doesn't return; someone else will get socked with it instead of you. Too bad for them, but at least you're rid of it. For now.

Let's take a more pleasant item of attention, like a new car. If you focus on the car you want, and keep focusing and keep focusing, you'll get it. But if you focus on the fact that it hasn't come yet, or the lack of it, *or how you can't afford it,* then that's exactly what you'll attract: a whole lot more "no car."

So you say, "Well hell, that just proves this stuff makes no sense; I've been focusing for years on what I want, namely more money, and I still don't have it."

Right! Because first there's the subject of money, and then there's the subject of the *lack* of money! And guess what 99.9 percent of us have been focusing on most of our lives? Right again.

We get what we focus on. Focus on the *lack* of what we want, and we are guaranteed to get more of it because, through matching vibrations, *we magnetize it in.* Law of Attraction, pure and simple.

Four Steps to Break Out

So here it is again: The more we think about something with even feeble emotion, the bigger and more powerful that something becomes in our life, regardless of whether it's the lack of what we want, or the thing itself.

If we say, "I want perfect health," and think emotionally about perfect health all the time, we'll either have it now or it will be on its way. But if we say, "I don't want sickness," and think emotionally about that often enough, we're opting for ill health because our focus is on the sickness.

If we think a lot about wanting a new house and can feel ourselves in it, it's on its way. But if we're constantly saying, "I don't want to live in this place any more," we'll be sticking around for a while.

If we think emotionally about something long enough, whether it's something we want or something we don't want, it's going to be coming into our world, like it or not.

What comes to us has nothing to do with what we're doing physically, or how worthy we are, or how good we are, or what our nonexistent destiny may be. It has only to do with how we are vibrating! Which means feeling. Which means attracting. Period!

So here's what Mom and Pop never told us, because Mom and Pop never knew. And here's what every positive thinking book or motivational speaker has been romancing, but never quite tied the knot because they honestly didn't know either.

Here are the four steps to deliberate creation, the four steps that are guaranteed—that's right, *guaranteed*—to bring into your life whatever is your passion and much, much more. They are guaranteed because they are universal law, the basic principles from which all creation has sprung. Now they are yours, if you want them.

Step 1. Identify what you DON'T want
Step 2. From that, identify what you DO want
Step 3. Get into the feeling place of what you want
Step 4. Expect, listen, and allow it to happen

That's it. That's all there is to it. As you get into the swing of this remarkable new journey, things seem to magically change in every area of your life. Worries, concerns, doubts and fears go from a constant ever-present little hum to an uncommon occurrence in a matter of weeks, and you can actually see it and feel it happening every day.

Your health turns around. Your bank account fills up. Your relationships do whatever you'd like them to do. Sales close. Promotions happen. Life becomes a daily joy. It's real. You can see it working. And then you know, you genuinely know, the only one at the helm of your ship is you. It really, truly is...just you!

Victim No More

As we embark on this adventure of living the Law of Attraction, we come very soon to the rather disturbing conclusion that there truly is no such thing as a victim, and that continuing to play the game of being a victim to any thing or any body guarantees only continued discontent from the relentless emission of low vibrations.

Oh sure, the rest of the world is still doing it, blaming "them" for what happened rather than their feelings; blaming "circumstances" for their bad luck rather than their feelings; blaming the drunk on the freeway, or the rotten boss, or the economy, or God for messing them up, rather than their feelings.

We may have been taught, and therefore have believed that we live at the mercy of others, or fate, or luck, or chance; certainly that is what most people on this planet live by. But once you start to see the Law of Attraction in operation, you ultimately come to understand that there is no such thing as a victim; never has been, never will be. There is no good luck, bad luck, good fortune, or coincidence. There is no destiny, fate, or providence. There is no big judge in the sky keeping score on how right or wrong you've been. There is no karma from past lives nor penance. That's all victim stuff. And there is not a victim among us, only cocreators in thought and feeling, powerful magnets attracting like bees to honey the matching frequency of our ever-flowing vibrations.

You never again have to believe that circumstances outside of you control your life. You never again have to believe that it is wrong to want. You never again have to believe that some great power outside yourself is pulling the strings, or that anyone or anything other than you is in control. You never again have to be afraid of "them" or "it," no matter who or what they may be, unless you so choose.

So how did we got in this mess? You got it! Eight billion people (plus however many more there have been over countless centuries) being born into vulnerable, lackful, fearful vibrations, all focusing on what they don't want and getting more of it.

It was never intended to be that way, but in our anxious state of needing to find a reason why things never seemed to go the way we wanted them to, we figured it had to be the fault of some factor separate from us: the government, the economy, our boss, our marriage, our background, our education, our rotten luck, even God.

Or maybe it was because we weren't worthy, didn't measure up, were too filled with sins, hadn't been fully put to the test, or had not in some way or other paid our rightful dues.

The reality — the *real* reality — is that we are already worthy, there is no test to pass, and sin is nothing but a man-made abomination to foster control by others.

The *real* reality is we have come here to thrive, and prosper, and live this grand human experience in light-hearted joy, not in struggle and pain. We have come here to have fun while we learn, to grow without suffering, and to harvest our desires in the absolute knowledge that we can have it all once we learn how to handle our energies...meaning...our emotions.

We came here with a guaranteed freedom of choice mandated by the very nature of our existence. The time has come for us to exercise that birthright. We are caught in no one's web. We are bound by no circumstance. We are victims to no conditions. Rather, we are beings who possess the sacred ability to implement any outlandish desire our limitless minds can concoct, for we possess unregulated, unrestricted, uncontested freedom of choice, no matter what those choices may be.

It's wake up time. It's time we remembered how to make those choices happen. It's time to take our heads

25

out of the sand and accept that it's no accident we get what we get in life. It's time for us to stop creating from the improper default setting and remember the secrets of the ancient wisdom we once knew so well before recorded history, wisdom that allowed us to create our passions with simple intent. It is time.

You deserve it all. You deserve to have all of your aspirations realized, no matter what they may be. You have only to want it and *feeeeel* it, and a whole new life of extraordinary happiness will be yours. Not can be; *will* be! That is a cosmic guarantee.

our magic genie

The process of creation is the same everywhere, whether it's a star system or designer jeans. Give thought to something you've infused with the appropriate feeling...which creates the appropriate vibration...and here it comes.

All the positive thoughts in the world won't make any difference, nor being a good person with a generous heart, nor praying, visualizing and meditating 'til dawn, nor even knocking our heads against countless stone walls in our fervent attempts to capture life-long dreams. None of that will create a thing until we launch the magnetic vibration to pull those dreams in through our infallible magic genie called feelings, that electro-magnetic authority of which dreams are made.

Just Two Kinds

You can take every book ever written on the subject of feelings and emotions, every class ever taught on the dark Freudian mysteries of the mind, every counseling group that has ever attempted to get us in touch with that obscure inner child, and anyone else trying to show us how to emancipate those frightening things we call feelings, and boil all the fancy techniques down to one simple remedy for creating an abundant and fulfilling life:

Learn to identify a good feeling from a bad feeling.

That's it. Learn to do that and you've got the course made. You can create anything your heart desires.

This is the secret that transforms us into deliberate creators instead of creators by accident. This is the power that changes wishful thinking into actuality, the simple art of being able to identify a good feeling from a bad one. That's all there is to it; end of lesson.

Don't worry, these kinds of feelings have nothing to do with digging up garbage from your past, or confronting whatever bogeymen might be currently residing in your emotional closet. They're just the garden variety type of feelings we have all day long. But once you learn to keep track of which ones feel good and which ones feel less than good, you're home free.

This is the nitty gritty. This is what "good luck" is all about. This is what closes the big sale, gets the beach-front house, fosters good health, brings spiritual fulfillment, and puts comfortable sums in the bank! Just learn to tell a wonderful feeling from an everyday downer one, and watch the magic happen.

Swallowing Glass

Feelings, those things we're all so terrified of if they happen to be negative, are nothing more than electromagnetic charges of energy that go zipping through our body, set off by our thoughts. The only reason we go to such lengths to avoid them is that some of those negative emotions don't feel so hot. We don't like the sensation they give us. So we stuff them way down deep where we think we don't have to deal with them anymore, and where, frankly, they're raising holy hell with our magnetics.

For now, let's just look at the ones we're aware of that don't get buried, starting with our everyday Feel Bad habit. That could mean anything from flat-lining (which is our normal daily state of neither up nor down, just existing) to a little bit down, to rip-roaring rage.

We feel *bad* when we think any kind of thought that doesn't have to do with joy, like guilt, loneliness, anger, resentment, worry, doubt, frustration, stress, even mild concern. Those are all fear-based thoughts that vibrate within us at an extremely low frequency, which is why they don't feel good. They are totally contrary to our high-frequency natural state.

On the other hand, we feel *good* when we think thoughts that have to do with joy, such as appreciation, delight, pleasure, exhilaration, enthusiasm, reverence, awe, gratitude, love, all those warm fuzzies we relish when they happen. The reason those thoughts feel so good to us is because they vibrate at a high frequency, which most definitely *is* our natural state.

No one can swallow cut up glass and expect to feel good, yet that's what we do all day with our somber thoughts and feelings. We literally bathe ourselves in unconscious negative energy (from our own thoughts as well as everyone else's)...which is totally contrary to our natural state of joy...which is why we rarely ever feel pumped up. We can't. Not as long as we're swimming all day in the low-frequency energy that we think is perfectly normal.

So it becomes a vicious circle: Both our conscious and unconscious day-to-day feelings, that we think are normal, are sending unnatural negative vibrations throughout our body...which make us feel down, or blah, or as though we are simply existing, or like we have no feelings at all. Since all of those feelings are various degrees of low-frequency energy flow, and since all we're putting out are low-frequency vibes, then low-frequency, second-rate events is all we're attracting back. Which makes us feel down...which puts out more low-frequency vibrations...which pulls in more low-frequency circumstances...which makes us feel down. And around and around and around we go.

Pat's Smiles

A couple of years ago in one of my weekend seminars on the Law of Attraction, there was an attractive, thirty-fivish gal (I'll call her Pat) who just couldn't seem to stop being nice. Goody-two-shoes nice.

She complimented me on my clothes (I wear sweat-shirts and jeans with holes at these seminars). She drooled verbal gratuities all over the cook. She was forever praising the participants for their heartfelt candor as they would correlate certain unpleasant happenings of their past to their bummed-out feelings of their present. For someone so overtly sunny, this gal was getting on my low-vibrational nerves.

After the first night's session was through and we had had our before-bed snack, Pat left the dining room, walked right into the big cigarette ash can placed outside the door, and fell flat on her face into a puddle of mud. She got up all cheery. Something was definitely wrong here.

The next day it was Pat as usual: compliments, praise, perpetual little smiles, and more accidents. She bumped into a chair in the dining room, spilling her fresh cup of coffee into someone's plate. She swallowed a candy the wrong way during someone's truly poignant story and had to be given the punch-in-the-stomach maneuver, after which she couldn't seem to stop nodding her appreciation toward the bear of a guy who had saved her life. Pat wasn't an accident waiting to happen; she was a perpetual accident in progress.

Finally, with prodding from the participants, Pat's story began to unfold. She came from a deeply religious family in which "being good" was what you did. The dictator of this stern way of life was her dad, who was also the minister of their church and a third generation minister at that! So this "show only goodness to the world, no matter how you feel" was so deeply ingrained in her by her dad, Pat truly believed this to be appropriate behavior. And it might have been, had it not been for the strong inner feelings of animosity that went along with her smiles.

"I used to hate having to be so proper and flattering all the time, especially to my elders," she said quietly during one session. "Complimenting adults terrified me, but I had to do it. All the time, I had to do it."

Pat's current life was this side of a mess. Though she had a college degree, she never moved beyond her entry level wherever she worked. She'd already been through three marriages and had enough accident claims to have her auto insurance cancelled. Her life had been more extreme than most, yet most of us could relate in one way or another. With her permission, we began to dissect her life as it related to her feelings.

The results were stunning. It didn't take long for everyone to see how Pat's long-standing yet hidden feelings of confusion, hostility, and unworthiness had created a constant outpouring of very low vibrations with every compliment or smile she emitted. And she got it! In no time at all, she could see the direct correlation between what she had been flowing out and the results she had been magnetizing back into her life. "Yuck out, yuck back," someone said. And she could see it clearly.

Pat has kept in touch and told me of a new excitement in her life that is bringing her more rich rewards than she ever dared to dream. She has stopped trying to please everyone except herself, and has even ventured into offering a few criticisms now and then. She tells me she smiles only when she means it, and compliments only when she feels sincere.

Today Pat is head of her own substance abuse recovery house. She's been with the same guy now for two years and hasn't so much as tapped another car.

What we flow out is what we get back. Pat has had to work hard at changing her negative out-flow, and while the negative emotions are not 100% gone, (they never will be for any of us), her predominant feelings of appreciation and gratitude (as opposed to being hopeless and luckless) have irrevocably transformed her life.

The feelings we flow out become the tangibles we attract back. It's that simple

What Makes Feelings

Most of us have this crazy notion that we just sort of popped into this place quite by accident. Not hardly. We each came with a partner, this profoundly loving, exclusive chaperone whom we have, by and large, chosen to ignore. Call it Inner Being, Higher Self (I really dislike that one), Expanded Self, God Self, or Mickey Mouse; call it what you will, it's that greater part of us we're attached to that comes with the physical package. We can't be physical without it, for it's the source that keeps us alive (not Living, perhaps, but alive). It is the pure positive energy of All That Is, of which we are a part; the pure positive energy of Life, which we are.

Didn't you ever feel like there's some secret part of you that knows everything there is to know but just doesn't stick its head out? There is. It's that broader, older, wiser part, that vastly expanded extension of each of us that communicates with us in the only way it knows...through feelings!

This expansion of ourselves that we came in with vibrates solely in a place which to us would feel like nirvana (and then some!), *waaaaay* up there on the frequency scale. In fact, that part of us wouldn't know a vibration of lack or stress if it tripped over it in a black hole. But if *we* were vibrating that fast, we wouldn't stay physical, so we get as close as we can with the high vibrations of plain old joy, exhilaration, appreciation, elation, all those luxurious sensations that equate to happiness and well-being. Which is why it feels so good to feel good. *You're vibrating closer to your real Self.* You and your nonphysical Self are in sync, plugged in together in that marvelous high frequency and all it has to offer.

So when we feel good, we're vibrating faster, the way we were designed to do. We're no longer recycling any of the low vibrational fear-based stuff we live in that's so utterly foreign to the body. We're in that space where we can get answers and Guidance, because now we're vibrationally walking hand in hand with the Self we really are.

By the same token, if we're sending out vibrations of lack or worry, the kind that make us feel anything other than joyful, we've pulled the plug from that unseen partner, and now everything is working at crossed purposes, and feels that way. It's like giving a youngster a big, fluffy new teddy bear, then snatching it away. Youngster isn't going to feel too hot about being disconnected from the thing which gives it so much joy.

So when we feel good, we're connected, vibrating closer to the higher frequency of our Expanded Selves. When we feel bad, or down, *or not much of anything,* we're disconnected and flowing the foreign vibrations of low frequency negativity throughout our bodies. In other words, if it's not about joy, it is *always* negative. If it's not about joy, we've swallowed cut glass.

The good news is we don't have to watch our thoughts every second of every day to get our lives back on track. Man, we'd go bonkers! All we have to do is stay tuned to how we're feeling, up or down, good or bad.

Ahhh's from the Gut

A somewhat extreme but amusing example of keeping track of our feelings came from a gal who was a session singer. I don't remember her name, only that she looked as if she'd been around the block more than a few times.

We were recording a group of songs a friend of mine had written for an elementary educational program my company was producing. I had never done any studio recording before, so everything that was going on was new and exciting. I was having a ball.

Our arranger had suggested we get some session singers for this one song. Since I didn't have a clue what he was talking about, he explained that they were a small group of singers who could create background harmony in a style that would fit most any song, giving a fuller, more professional sound to the piece.

Amazing! How could a group of people...who didn't know the music...who had no idea what the program was about...create a sound amongst themselves that would mesh with the theme and music? Oh well, I guessed I'd find out.

When the troupe of three arrived, I was doubtful. They were too quick. They each looked at the music individually, chatted a bit, nodded to each other, then said, "Okay Sam, we're ready any time you are."

Excuse Me, Your LIFE Is Waiting

Huh??? How could they be?! No practice? No chatting with the arranger? No asking me, the boss?

The intro started, the soloist was at the mike, and our session singers were behind her with their own mike, presenting this sort of nonchalant confidence.

After our soloist did her first bit, one of the session singers jumped right in to take over the next verse. We were all startled, but my God, it sounded terrific. Then the three of them were humming, then "ahhhing," then "ooooing," then "mmming," and then all of a sudden singing the words in harmony right behind the soloist.

I was dumbfounded. Our arranger smiled. My friend who had written the song was open-mouthed. Our soloist was elated. The guys in the booth were smiling and shaking their heads. And the one session gal who had looked like worn-out leather now looked twenty years younger. One take and we had it. Just one take. Impossible! Incredible!

As the singers were about to leave, I went up to the older gal who was obviously the leader and asked her how they did that. How could they jump in, not knowing the music, and create a better feel than what we had ever envisioned in the first place? And in one take?

"Oh, it's no biggie, hon," the gal said, in her almost bass voice. "We've been doing this for so long, we know what "oooo's" go where. And the harmony's no problem. The only thing that's ever a problem is my gut."

"Say again?"

"Well, if it's all fitting together, I feel like I'm sailing to the moon. My gut feels all excited like when I'm streaking down a roller coaster. But if I don't have that feeling, we can do a hundred takes and not one will ever be right, even if it sounds okay to the producer. It just won't be right. It's gotta be that joy, that's all; just pure joy from my gut. Then I know we've got it. This time, it came right away on the first take, and I knew we were done. So did everybody else. It was just pure joy, and I could feel it in every cell of my body. I always do. You know what I mean?"

No, I surely did not know what she meant, though I do now. This rough and tumble gal had no idea that what she was experiencing was the actual vibrational shift from low to high frequency energy surging throughout her body. Nor did she create it on purpose, as we'll learn to do. All she knew was that she could feel something very special happen inside her when her group clicked in, and she rightly called the sensation "pure joy."

Now granted, the kind of Feel Good/Feel Bad awareness I've been talking about may be a whole lot more subtle than hers, but unlike her joy sensations which only happened when everything outside of her jibed just right, we're going to learn to click-in joy at will.

Original Intent, Our Treasure Map of Desire

As self-serving at it may sound, we came here to this blessed planet with only one intent: to find ways to feel good most of the time, not just some of the time.

That singular intent—to feel good—is built into each and every one of us, and if we'll just pay attention to it, we'll have a personally engraved treasure map to happiness. Here's why:

When we're having good feelings about anything, it means we're on track with our Original Intent—to feel good, to be happy, and to vibrate way up there. It means we're on track toward something we've long wanted or even recently wanted. Either way, having it come our way will make us happy. We're on track toward something we believe will enhance our life, therefore make us feel better, therefore raise our frequencies, therefore bring us closer to our natural state, which is the whole challenge of our being here.

So here's the key: Original Intent always manifests as desire...desire for anything that will get our passion going, be it a new red Ferrari or a desire to live in harmony with all life. It might show up as a new desire for a clean garage, to learn western dancing, or to run an old-fashioned hardware store in the country. Or it could be an old desire to live by the beach, or learn to play the piano. Either way, it's a desire, something we want.

Where we get into such trouble with our desires, though, is the hang-ups we have about them, because, depending on the nature of the desire, society has a way of calling us selfish if we pursue them. Yet if we're really following those inner urges—which will make us happy simply because we believe they will—we're following our Original Intent to have fun while we're here and learn whatever it is we came here to learn in the vibration of joy, not struggle. That's hardly self-serving.

But society's pressure is unrelenting, causing us all too often to succumb to our "shoulds" by heading us off in the opposite direction of our happiness-making desires. Now we're off course, which is, sadly, where most of us live most of the time. We've veered away from our Original Intent by vibrating in the low frequency of social-conscious fear-based stuff. While that frequency might not cause us to feel rotten, we surely won't be bubbling over with merriment. We couldn't be; one frequency is a downer (social consciousness), and the other is an upper (Original Intent). They will never mix.

So now if we stay on that off-course path, disallowing our own joy, demanding altruism of ourselves, depriving ourselves of our Original Intent, we've joined the multitudes righteously following their hated low-frequency "shoulds" instead of their high-frequency joys. Needless to say, the results of that kind of relentless energy flow on this planet have not been pretty.

Red Flag/Green Flag

Let's go back to your wanting a new car. And let's say the car you have right now is in pretty good shape, so you don't have any pressing need to have new wheels, just a deep desire. In fact, for as long as you can remember, you've had this passion for a spiffy little red convertible with wire wheels. (If you live in Alaska and can't stand red, play the game with me anyhow.)

But where in the hell is it? You've had this desire for ages. You've been thinking and thinking about it off and on for years, so how come it's not parked in your garage? Here's why:

You're zipping along on the freeway one day, and sure enough, there's your dream car right in front of you. You groan from envy because you think you can't afford it. The yearning starts. You look at the car with great longing and shake your head in a "Man, wouldn't it be nice" kind of discouragement. Instead of feeling all jazzed at seeing your dream car, you're feeling sunk, accompanied with that knee-jerk reaction of "Oh hell, forget it."

Which is precisely why it's not parked in your garage.

You're focusing on the *lack* of your car rather than the joy of having it. You're sending out such a bunch of negative Feel Bad vibrations, your Expanded Self is waving big Red flags and shouting, "Hey, friend, you're feeling snarley because you're focusing on the fact that you don't have the car. Keep thinking like that and you're sure to get more of the same, a whole lot more No Car. If you really want the thing, start feeling good when you think about it, then watch what happens."

You've just been given a Red flag warning in the form of a gloomy feeling called negative emotion. The warning says you're focusing on something you don't want—the *lack* of having the car—all because of your perception that you can't afford it.

That downer feeling is a Red flag, your clue that the way you're flowing your energy (thinking and feeling about it) is guaranteed to keep your car away. So now all you have to do is change the way you think and feel about that car (your desire), and it's yours.

We flow this sort of downer-feeling energy out from us every day, which is why we've gotten precious little of what we ever hoped to have. We see something we've wanted in life (which could be anything from an expensive red car to understanding quantum physics), and from our position of lack—meaning that we don't have it and aren't real sure we can ever get it—our focus and feelings are squarely on *what we don't have.* So that's all we'll ever magnetize in...more "don't have." The law of physics never changes; we get what we focus on.

Yearning for, wishing for, longing for, even hoping for are not activities of focusing on what we want. They're just negative thoughts that vibrate from a place of discouragement, a place of lack born from the pessimistic beliefs that we'll probably never have what we want. And with those kinds of feelings flowing out, we won't.

We get what we focus on; focus on the lack of something, and that's what we're guaranteed to get, because what the universe gives us, in every moment of every day, corresponds precisely with what we are vibrating.

The bottom line is this: If we're not feeling up when we think about something, we're flowing some degree of negative emotion, a Red flag warning telling us to pay attention to what we're sending out.

In our playful example of your red car, if what you're feeling when you think about it isn't giving you some kind of emotional high, some sort of goose-bumpy turn-on, some kind of neat buzz, some kind of warm fuzzy, some kind of rush, or some kind of delight in *any* form, then you're feeling and projecting just the opposite: negative vibrations from your frustration over not having the car.

From our focus on lack, we can never attract the opposite. To attract whatever it is we want into our life, we have to change our focus, which will change our feelings, which will change our vibrations.

Getting Your Car

Okay, let's get this snafu turned around now so that red car can be yours. Back to our original formula:

1) You identify what you DON'T want. (You don't want any more of not having the red car.)
2) You identify what you DO want. (That's easy.)
3) You get into the feeling place of what you want. (That's where we are now.) Then,
4) You expect, listen, and allow it to happen.

Now, instead of wishing or yearning for the car when you see it or think about it—which only makes you feel lousy anyhow—start appreciating that little sweetie. Appreciate its style, its wheels, its interior, its speed, its ego appeal. That is most surely going to make you feel—and vibrate—a whale of a lot faster and higher than focusing on the lack of it all. And it's only the high vibration that will reel it in, not the low.

Let's keep going.

As you bathe in the all-encompassing pride of your soon-to-be acquisition, and drink in the opulent new-car smells, and mirror-like finish, and out-of-this-world sound system, all of your increasingly magnetic vibrations are totally positive, which means you're sending out a powerful new signal that's creating an unobstructed pathway for your desire to magnetize itself into your world.

In fact, with all those up-up-up vibes you're sending out, you're a veritable walking high-frequency magnet, feeling really really good, flying *Green flags* of Feel Good all over the place. Your feelings are in agreement with your Original Intent to have fun. You've stopped attracting more of what you *don't* want and are now seriously attracting what you *do* want. (Never mind how you're going to pay for it, that's not your job to figure out). As long as you stop focusing on the fact that it's not parked in your garage yet, your spiffy little red dream is definitely on its way.

Negative feelings, which come from thoughts of "don't have," "can't have," or "never will have," are simply not in agreement with your Original Intent. (And neither are your "shoulds.") It's so simple: Put glum feelings out, and you're going to get glum circumstances back.

If, on the other hand, you allow yourself to be turned on by thinking about your dream car, and insist to yourself that things are now in the process of turning around—*no matter what you may see in front of you to the contrary!!!*—then those positive thoughts will ultimately magnetize in your desires. They must; it's the physics of the universe.

Remember, it's the *feeeelings* that will do it, not the thoughts alone. It's the *feeeelings* that create the magnetism and the vibration in the waves we send out. It's the feelings, the feelings, the feelings...that come from our thoughts!

Good Old Media

A few nights ago while I was fixing dinner, I switched on the local TV news and almost threw up before I had even tasted a bite of food.

First came the report of the latest outbreak of some weird strain of flu, so exotic, in fact, that it was doubtful the most powerful flu shots could defeat it.

"In Blah Blah town, 1,500 miles away, it's been reported that three out of five residents have been severely stricken with this uncontrollable new virus."

Terrific! Now probably four out of five watching the show will start focusing their fears and "don't want" emotions on this tacky little bug, which will absolutely insure its growth and make it ripe for being sucked into anyone with a matching fearful frequency. What might have been nothing more than a few sniffles around town without the TV report is now plainly going to be a mess.

But that was only the first part of the local evening news. Next (so help me, this is a true story!) was a report on a new incident of hamburger food poisoning discovered outside the city, and the concern was being voiced about the recovery of the children now being hospitalized, since the last time this happened, some of the youngsters didn't make it.

Oh good! Now we'll have thousands of parents waving big Red flags, flowing fearful charges of negative vibrations (like terrified) to that one poor little piece of bacteria until it and all the sad events that get sucked in with it—that everyone wanted to avoid—will blow up into reality. (It did. Half a dozen deaths were attributed to that bacteria within a month.)

By this time I was getting mad, and starting to realize that my own feelings were hardly of a joyous nature. Right out loud I stormed, "Okay, okay, Expanded Self, I hear you; this ain't making me feel good. I'll turn the fool thing off." But not before the last item I heard was about an elderly woman who had just been found raped and murdered. By that time I was furious, feeling awful, and wondering just how many elderly women would get it in the next few days through events ignorantly magnetized into their reality by focusing their own titanic fears on what they wanted most to avoid.

We hear it all the time from our media: another bombing, another arson, another rash of some awful bug. So everybody focuses on the awfulness of the happening, which just serves to magnetize in more of the same.

Did they have guns in school, and gang rapes, and buildings being blown up, and serial arsonists in 1865? No, because they didn't have the media to create the focus to cause the vibrations to bring it about en masse. Instead, they had newspapers and posters about their train robbers and bank robbers, so what they got more of was train robberies and bank robberies.

Trust me, the Law of Attraction was just as active in Billy the Kid's time as it is today, because it's the fundamental law of creation throughout the universe. Focus with repeated intense emotion on something we don't want (or do want), and sooner or later that something is going to be in our lap.

The 18-Wheeler Syndrome

Of course, there aren't two kinds of energy, one that makes us feel good, and one that makes us feel rotten. But there are varying degrees of Feel Good vibrations and Feel Bad vibrations to any thought we send out. We'll call them positive energy and negative energy, even though it's all the same, just vibrating differently.

Every time we think of anything, we're flowing some kind of positive or negative energy (feeling) toward whatever it is we're thinking about, and the litany never changes: as we think, we feel; as we feel, we vibrate; as we vibrate, we attract. Then we get to live the results.

But how do those so-called results really get to us? What's the routine that causes us to step into something we've been thinking about?

In your young and reckless days, did you ever set out for some dumb and stupid fun by driving too close to the back end of an 18-wheeler? Tuck the nose of your car right up to a big truck's rear end and I guarantee you'll get the picture fast! You can take your foot off the gas pedal, lean back and relax, and be sucked right along to the truck's destination. I'm hardly advocating such moronic behavior, but the principle of attraction is the same.

Two things are going on each time we think seriously about something. First is the vibration that is set up from the feeling the thought evokes (happy, sad, etc.). Second is the activation by our emotions of little specks of thought I call thought particums. Once these magnetic specks are activated by our feelings, they are instantly programmed to magnetize in accord with whatever it was we were vibrating.

So we think about something, and think about it some more, and talk about it, and mull it over the next day, and the next and the next until pretty soon there are so many of those same-frequency thoughts flitting around out there, they start clumping together like dough balls. The more thoughts we send out of the same kind, the bigger these clumps grow until they become expanding clusters of awesome magnetic power big enough to form their own immensely powerful whirlpools of magnetic energy, either positive (happy) or negative (bummer) in nature.

These power centers, vortexes of monumental magnetic energy, now draw into their whirling centers anything and everything of similar vibrations—including you—which will eventually cause events to happen. Before you know it, you've been sucked right into the middle of some happening you initiated with your recurring thoughts and feelings. It might be the thing you were focusing on, or it might be something *completely different, yet made up of the same vibrations*. Although we can certainly flow feelings without thought, in our example it's the repetitive thinking that has set up the repetitive feelings that has started the magnetic ball rolling.

The critical point to remember here is that the more we think about anything, whether it's something we want in our lives or something we don't want, the faster we're going to magnetize it into our experience. That, in a nutshell, is the universal Law of Attraction: "That which is like unto itself is drawn."

The Power of You

We've been raised in a society that has been flowing energy helter-skelter for countless centuries, being unconsciously sucked along in back of a whole lot of 18-wheelers that were not headed anywhere near where we wanted to go.

There are no victims here, just flow-ers of energy; in our case, flowing right into the unfortunate forgetfulness that we've always had the power to create our lives and our world however we damn well wanted it to be. Instead, from our lack of understanding energy flow, we became masterfully adept at creating by default.

Although the process of becoming a deliberate creator is extraordinarily simple, it's not always easy, for the concept is far and away too foreign to us. The idea that we've been creating our world by feeling alone—whether manufactured from thought or from ongoing emotions—will most likely be highly suspect at first. To realize that we have always had the power to do this creation thing any time we choose, in any manner we want, could certainly be disheartening and even beyond our willingness to accept...for a while.

Nevertheless, physics is physics, magnetism is magnetism, and both tell us "that which is like unto itself is drawn." Whether it's a nebula, a black hole, or a human being wading through physical existence, that's the way it works.

But we don't have to chew on all this newness by ourselves, for we are not alone on this ride. We each have a profoundly loving partner of incomprehensible knowledge, beauty, and power, a greatly Expanded Self, an Inner/Outer Being to whom we are irrevocably joined for this physical ride, a Being whose devoted support never leaves us, and whose Guidance is as tangible as the last emotions we just experienced, those precious jewels we call *feelings, feelings, feelings,* the magic genie of all creation.

no, no, not that

(Step One)

I was driving down the freeway one day listening to a favorite Neal Diamond tape, not focused on much of anything, when I realized I had one of those funny little knots in my stomach, the kind that feels like there's a serious hole in your gut with a not-so-gentle breeze sailing through. Something was off base somewhere, and good old Expanded Self was sending me a clear signal to pay attention to my feelings. But since nothing came to mind, I decided to ignore it.

Big mistake!

I let my thoughts wander, paying little attention to the very obvious Red Flag I was feeling. Sure enough, my meandering thoughts wandered right into one of the loans I was in the process of closing. At that time I was running my own mortgage company, a business that finds the best interest rates for people who want to buy or refinance their homes, and then arranges for the funding and ultimate closing of the loan.

We were almost ready to close this young couple's loan when some sticky problems showed up I wasn't sure I could solve. That in itself was bad enough so near the finish line, but the worst of it was that these kids were really counting on this loan to end some of their grisly financial troubles. So here's my focus 100% on what I do not want to happen (the loan to fall through), I've got Red Flags of negative feelings flying all over the place—a little dread, a little guilt, a large helping of gloom—and I'm ignoring them! The results of that negative energy flow was immediate.

I had about one more mile of music before the tape player started eating my "Jonathan Livingston Seagull" cassette. About two miles after that I was squeezed right into a four-lane traffic jam from daytime road work. About twenty minutes and another mile after that, I get rear-ended (just rear-bumped) by some dude farther away in mad-land than I was. About ten minutes after that, I spilled the rest of my coffee all over a file of original loan papers. And when I finally got out of that mess and made it to a telephone, the lender told me the loan had fallen through.

Considering how I had been flowing my energy, I was hardly surprised. I knew exactly what had happened, what a dork I'd been, and exactly what I had to do...fast!

What had happened? What had caused that whole chain of pesky events? Was it just coincidence, a nasty string of unlucky circumstances? Not on a bet! It's how every single one of us has been creating our days since nursery school, focusing on all the stuff around us we didn't like, didn't want, and feeling helpless as we watched it get worse.

We've been living a life we felt was largely at the mercy of forces outside of ourselves over which we had no control. I mean, how many of us would take credit for having a lousy boss, being robbed, getting laid off, or catching the flu? And how many of us would not blame the government, or the economy, or our families, or the "system" for all that's wrong in our lives? Oh sure, we'll take credit for some of it, the things we've set out to do...and did. But would we honestly be willing to take responsibility for every last thing that's ever happened to us? Not likely!

What's Wrong Is What's Wrong

There's a world of closet sufferers walking around this planet who will swear to you on their new Toyotas that they hardly ever have a negative thought.

They'll tell you their life is just fine, and that they're quite happy. Yet these are the same people who will tell you that life is never fair, it's full of trials, and that we must all learn to take our share of knocks. But yes, they're quite happy, thank you. Never got all they might have liked, but we must take life as it is dealt. So yes, they're quite content.

To which I say "Bull!"

We cannot flow negative energy of any kind, in any degree, in any amount, and be happy. And that means anything from mild irritation, to normal no-feeling (flat-lining), to perpetual dread. It is a physiological impossibility to be happy with that kind of energy flowing out, because we're flowing two different vibrations that activate two different external (and internal) results.

Closet sufferers are victims, plain and simple, just as most of us have been at one time or another, viewing our world as the result of uncountable circumstances over which we believed we had no control. We've all been there, or are there. It's only a matter of how much of the victim myth we've chosen to buy into and live.

But we don't have to stay there. In fact, once you start to really see this magnetics business in action, it becomes pretty hard to ignore the glaring evidence: our lives have been molded by the daily flow of our energy, not by luck, fate, circumstance, or a rich uncle.

When you stop to think that we've spent decades questioning what's wrong with everything, therefore focusing on all the things in our world we didn't like, didn't want, or wanted to change, it's little wonder we've attracted such a barrelful of trials. No human being can be so continually disconnected from their Source energy and get to wherever it is they want to go.

So here's the flash: continuing to live life as a victim of circumstance, forever focusing on what's wrong with everything and everybody, will never, ever, bring the life desired. It will only bring one thing: more of whatever it is we're wanting so desperately to change.

Recipe for Creation

The recipe for creating anything is really quite simple. Take good or bad feelings (meaning positive or negative vibrations), bake with varying degrees of emotion to increase magnetism, and here comes what we've attracted, like it or not. What we have focused on, and how we have vibrated about it, is what we have gotten...from birth.

So if we've been in a constant search for ways to fix all the things around us we don't like, or even if we have allowed them to be there but still haven't liked them, then we've been in a constant state of focusing on what we haven't wanted. For years!

It takes only sixteen seconds to link up vibrationally to whatever we're focusing on. That's right, only sixteen seconds of pure, focused thought, good or bad, negative or positive. In that brief time, we start to vibrate on the same frequency as whatever it is we've been emotionally thinking about, which means we're ripe for attracting that thing, if we keep it up. Needless to say, we've all had an oceanful of things we've thought about over and over in repetitious sixteen second segments, all those vibrations of frustration, and tension, and concern over the countless things we didn't want, didn't like, couldn't handle, didn't know what to do with, or thought we had to put up with. Which is why, for most of our lives, we've continued to attract more of the same. Charming!

Up to now, that's the fundamental way we've sculpted our lives, by this ceaseless attention to all the things we could do without, producing an unceasing undertow of negative tension.

Remember, I'm not talking daily rage here, just that perpetual silent murmur of "gotta fix it, gotta do it better, gotta make it right, gotta find a way" that's called either quiet concern or Knot-in-Gut.

And on the other side of the same coin, it's called "gotta accept it, gotta live with it, nothing I can do about it, like it or not." Same thing, same vibrations.

This is why it is so important for us to have a broad understanding of just what negative emotion is, how covertly it works, how to spot it, why we keep having it, and, oddly enough, how truly vital it is to the process of taking control.

So please don't look at this chapter on "Negative" as negative. It's the secret component of getting us where we want to go.

Toys 'R' Yours

Imagine being a youngster turned loose in the biggest, brightest toy store you've ever seen in this whole wide world, and being told you can help yourself to whatever you wanted. Wow! It's almost too far out to imagine, yet that's what our universe is, one gigantic toy store where anything we've ever wanted to play with is either already there for the pickin's, or waiting to be created. All we have to do is *feeeeel* what we want and magnetize it in.

Let's say, for example, that here in your magic toy store there's an exciting new job waiting for you. Or maybe it's your next house, the one with every conceivable luxury and more silly gadgets than you've ever seen. Around the corner there's a fantastic new relationship (or a polished-up old one), and hot dog! There's your up-dated body with all the appropriate corrections.

This is terrific! But where are all of these goodies going to come from? Are they just going to fall from the sky or come from our guardian angels in the outfield? No, they're going to come from you. To pull them in, all you have to do is want them with a gut-blasting, Feel Good vibration.

Moldy Old Beliefs

It's hard for us to swallow the concept that what has been in life has absolutely nothing to do with what can be. That's diametrically opposed to how we think things work. Yet what has been—or whatever is in our face right this minute—is simply the result of how we've flowed our energies in days gone by. It is not "the way things are."

What has been is not a result of anything or anybody "out there," nor is it a result of good or bad luck, a result of being a good person, a righteous person, or a sanctimonious ass. What has been has nothing to do with family, or government, or schooling.

What has been in our life comes squarely from where our focus has been. And a major part of our focus has come from antiquated beliefs, those smelly old philosophies that were pounded into our heads, or that we blindly accepted as reality from way back to toddler days. We were jammed full of them then and still are—archaic patterns of thought about what we think reality is, thought patterns that frankly belong in the garbage can.

Fussing Father Fred

One summer many years ago, I was dating an Episcopalian priest. For a long time I thought this guy was the be-all and end-all of the male race. He was tall, well built, handsome, about ten years my senior, bright, well educated, and came from a lovely New England family. Just my kind of guy.

Father Fred was a brilliant speaker, delivering educational as well as spiritual sermons, but his church was usually this side of empty. In an attempt to remedy the embarrassing situation, he would change his style, change his tone, change his organization of material, even change the altar dressings, but nothing seemed to work. People simply didn't like going to hear him nor being around him.

Those were carefree days for me. I was in my early twenties, hadn't really squared off on what I wanted to do with my life, and was finding my drinking to be more and more enjoyable. Since Father Fred apparently found the same degree of enjoyment in his imbibing, the two of us were having a blast.

But blast or no, something was beginning to rub me the wrong way. It was subtle, but never stopped. Over drinks, out for drives, immersed in parties, it seemed that no matter where we were or what we were doing, Fred was attacking something or someone in the church. It was as if he were obsessed. One night it would be a bishop, the next night it was something about his improper training, or low budgets, or the diocese's restrictions on "high" services. His attacks seemed endless. And they were starting to drive me nuts.

I was no psych student, but this was absurd. When I finally asked him about it, his very matter-of-fact response was, "That's the way I am. I have an ability to see what's wrong with things. The church is outdated and needs renovating, but it's not up to me to do it. I just have the talent to see what needs changing."

Pretty soon I could see that Fred approached everything in life as a grievance, not just the church.

The world was a mess, everything needed changing or fixing, but he was never the one to do it. In fact, he felt incapable of doing much of anything, which is why, I guessed, he was so obsessed with conducting his services as flawlessly as possible. There, at least, he felt he could excel, whether his church was empty or not.

But for all his blunderbuss, Fred was truly afraid of authority. "I can't because..." was his litany. He couldn't get a raise, a secretary, a better allowance for his parish, not even a guest speaker when he wanted to go away. He could only focus on the fact that it would never happen. So, of course, it didn't.

Poor Fred lived in a perpetual world of Don't Wants, believing the more he focused on them and stewed about them, the better chance he had of making them go away. He saw himself as a helpless victim required to submit to the greater powers that be who were waiting to snip his ecumenical rise in the bud. Looking back on it now, I can see why people didn't want to be around him. Although his sermons rarely reflected his negativity, folks intuitively picked up on his energy, and didn't want any part of it.

Again, this is an extreme example (they're the only ones I remember) of how most of us have lived, and yet...and yet?

These kinds of moldy old beliefs, such as the powerful ones Fred had concerning authority and fate, are our biggest roadblocks to purposeful creating because they come up and clobber us whenever we think we'd like to take another direction. You know the kinds I mean: you think you'd like to get a new job, and up shoots the highly charged emotional thought, "Oh I can't because..."

Or a new car: "Oh I can't, because..."

Or a new relationship: "Oh no, no, no, I REALLY can't, because..."

They are our ancestors' values and ethics about "shoulds" and "if onlys" and "rights and wrongs."

They are outdated philosophies from our religions that tell us we can't have a better life until we check out of here, or that "only through suffering can we hope to achieve the kingdom of God."

They are convictions about accomplishment and success and working and earning.

They are beliefs that have compelled us to look forever for what's wrong with everything, convinced we must find ways to fix it all before we can move ahead: the job, the environment, our mate, the government, the schools, our kids, and mostly...ourselves.

"Gotta fix it, gotta fix it, gotta fix it; don't want it this way, don't like it that way, gotta fix it."

Perhaps our most damaging beliefs, though, are the cherished ones we hold about how it's always the other guy's fault: our bonehead leaders, our drunken families, our horny boss. We blame with the constancy of the rising sun, thinking there's nothing wrong with that because that's how the world operates. We're certain that blaming makes us feel better, so we do it some more, and some more, and some more, never having a clue how destructive such negative vibrations have been—and are being—to our lives.

But here's the good news: no matter what today's parade of psychologists and counselors say to the contrary, we do *not* have to dig up all that useless junk to make life work our way. With some simple tricks of the trade, and the awareness that this is really no more difficult than paying attention to how we're *feeeeeling*, we simply learn to override all that moldy old stuff that's kept us imprisoned for so long, living an arduous life that we always thought was perfectly normal.

Don't Wants

There's only one place negative energy—*all* negative energy—comes from: our Don't Wants. Sometimes we call it guilt; other times we call it fear, or blame, or worry, or doubt. But for now, so that we can stay out of all the hackneyed psychiatrists' junk, we're calling it all "Don't Wants."

Hard as it may be to believe, the majority of our daily thoughts—and therefore feelings—are about things we don't want: big and little, here and there, now, back then, and in the future. This kind of thinking is endless, mostly automatic and unconscious, and horrendously restraining. Take a look:

We don't want to drive to work in bad weather
We don't want to be late to work
We don't want to displease the boss
We don't want to have the drought continue
We don't want to buy bad meat at the store
We don't want to look bad
We don't want to have our kids hurt
We don't want to get the flu
We don't want to get fired
We don't want to stand in a long line

We don't want get up in the morning
We don't want any more bills
We don't want to live in such a cold climate
We don't want the light to turn red
We don't want to get a divorce
We don't want to fail the test. Etc., etc., etc., etc., etc., etc., etc., etc., etc.

Now, granted, one or two of those things listed are nothing but choices we're making in the moment, so they're not going to elicit much emotion from us, and therefore, not do much damage. But as inconsequential as the rest of those items may seem, they definitely are not. Focus on any one for any length of time, and you'll see it in your face before you know what hit you.

Even worse, the collective power of all the personal conscious and unconscious Don't Wants we spew out energetically all day long becomes the vibrational mixture that makes up our individual world. Like it or not, that mix is normally negative.

Take, for instance, all those stale cobwebs from our past, our "if onlys."

If only I had had different parents
If only I had gone to college
If only I hadn't married that one
If only I had taken that job
If only I hadn't switched lanes
If only, if only, if only...

If Onlys are simply the past tense of Don't Wants. "I didn't really want those parents." "I didn't want to have to search for work without a degree." "I didn't want an unhappy marriage." "I didn't want such a poor paying job." "I didn't want to get in a car accident, but I switched lanes."

And then there are all those tricky Negative Wants which are nothing more than Don't Wants in disguise.

I want to get well

I want to get out of debt

I want to lose weight

I want to stop smoking

I want our lousy marriage to shape up

I want my spouse to get a better job

You may think you're being positive by not stating a Don't Want, but where's your focus? It's taken dead aim on precisely what you Don't Want any more of in your life. And since we get what we focus on...*hello!* Here it comes to meet you.

Now I'd be the first to agree with you when you protest that you are *not* a negative person. Most of us are not—thank God—like Father Fred. We enjoy life the best we can. We thrill at the sight of a sunset. We toss small fish back into the water. We're pleased when friends get promoted. We laugh at our kids' unfunny jokes. We enjoy going out on Friday nights. We take pride in our accomplishments. We give credit where credit is due. We do what we can to bring joy into the lives of others as well as ourselves.

And yet, our endless life-focus has been on Don't Wants. We don't want to have to work so hard, we don't want our car to break down, we don't want this and don't want that all day long, which just magnetizes in more of whatever it is we're not wanting.

Let's say there's something about your job you don't like, or you drive a broken-down car, or you've got a mate who's driving you bonkers. And let's say you think about this Don't Want again and again. Well, each time you go back to that subject and add another sixteen seconds to it with some juiced-up emotions, you're not only growing it and adding more power to it, you're making it a whole lot easier to think about. Whoa!

Like cutting a trail in the jungle, you swack here, and swack there, and pretty soon you have a nice clean path on which to trek back and forth. So you do. On the same subject! You think about it, and think about it, and think about it until pretty soon it's so easy to think about, you can hardly get it out of your head. And before you know it, the very thing you haven't wanted to happen...has!

If you don't want—real bad—to have your new car nicked, you're a shoo-in to attract a matching vibration called "jerk-in-parking-lot."

If you don't want—real bad—unpleasant neighbors to move in next door, you're ripe for attracting nerds with barking dogs, and keeping them there.

If you don't want—real bad—any more problems with bills, those problems are sure to get worse.

If you don't want—real bad—to be alone for the holidays ...all right, you get the picture.

Whatever you include in your vibration for sixteen seconds or longer is on its way to you, whether you like it or not. So when you're talking about all the things you don't want, and flowing out only sixteen seconds of feeling each time you talk about one of them, that thing has now become a part of you, part of your everyday vibration. Pretty soon you're living it...not liking it at all

...vibrating it...talking about it...complaining about it ...stewing over it...and making it an even stronger match to your daily vibration than it was in the first place. You are vibrating with the very thing you do not want.

Now that thing can't leave you. It is part of you. No matter how much you keep grumbling over it or worrying about it, it cannot leave! It is now included within your everyday vibration. And the more you live it, focus on it, and brood over it, the stronger your vibration becomes to match and hold this thing you want so badly to get rid of.

There's More...

There's another problem. Remember the tuning forks where you ding one in a room and all others of a matching frequency ding right along too? The same thing happens with our thoughts. As you think more and more about something, you're not only attracting more of whatever it is you're thinking about, *you're dinging and pulling in anything else—ANYTHING else—that just happens to be on a similar frequency.*

The results could be anywhere from a bad case of flu to being fired, when what you were really thinking about was how you didn't have enough money to fix the roof. Now all of a sudden you're getting these cute little surprise packages *of the same vibration*—but not the same thing—as your Don't Want, and just as unwelcome. By thinking about one, you're sending out an open invitation to anything else that happens to be pinging on the same frequency. If it's a vibratory match, it can be yours, whether you were focused on it or not.

Didn't you ever notice that when one thing starts to go wrong, so does everything else? That's because the vibrations you're sending out are matching up with all sorts of different stuff on the same wave length. By your thinking about that one thing over and over again, you're creating a spiral of thought that has now been made considerably bigger with heaven-knows-what-else swirling around in its magnetic center and headed your way.

For instance, think long enough about how you dislike your job, and you end up having a fender-bender, your sink stops up, you lose your keys, your refrigerator blows out, and you stub your toe. All from thinking over and over about just one Don't Want...your job...which, by the way, is now a whole lot worse than it was before.

Don't Wants can be huge or trivial, but either way, when we're focused on one or a hundred and one, we've got negative currents streaming out of us that are most definitely not going to magnetize back anything even remotely close to joy. They can't. They're on a vastly different frequency.

And so around and around we go, existing; that's all, just existing, holding ourselves apart from the higher energies of bubbly well-being which is our true state, *and* our absolute, irrefutable right.

Two things are certain: 1) Think long enough about something you don't want, and either you're going to attract it, or it's going to attract you, and 2) Think about a Don't Want with any amount of feeling behind it, and you will automatically attract other lousy happenings of a similar frequency.

In Sync or Out

So what do we do about all that? How do we change it? We surely can't watch every little thing we say or do or think all day long.

Don't worry, it's not that tough. All we need to do is go back to our magic genie, feelings, and learn to identify how it feels to flow "this kind" of energy, or "that kind," and learn to recognize when we're feeling down or up, bad or good, zoned out with no feeling or *really* happy.

But let's back up here for a minute, to vibrations. Everything in the universe responds to vibrations; it is law. And with us here on this planet, that means touch, smell, color, taste, hearing, and...emotions.

When we feel joy, or passion, or love, or any other kind of exquisite happiness, those feelings are our interpretations of particular kinds of vibrations. On the flip side, when we feel feelings of anxiety, or guilt, or resentment, they, too, are interpretations of vibrations. And don't forget why one kind feels better than the other; one is close to our Source, the other is not.

We each are physical extensions of much, much more than what we see, extensions of a much more vast non-physical Being—our Source energy—that just happens to be expressing Itself, right now, in a human body. When we vibrate in sync with that energy, we feel good. And vice-versa: when we feel down, it's because we are vibrating out of sync with that pure, positive energy.

Don't Wants mean we are out of sync. As we look at something and say "I don't want this," two things happen.

First, there's no way that Don't Want can possibly go away, because we're holding it in our vibration by our very attention to it. And second, we feel bad, down, low, nothing at all, or any other kind of feeling that is anything but happiness.

And so, the more in sync we are with our Source energy, the better we feel. And the more out of sync with our Source energy we are, the worse we feel. Or let's put it another way: feeling good is natural, but not normal to us right now. Anything less than that is unnatural, and sadly, quite normal to us right now.

But Beware

Our primary problem with negative emotion is that we rarely think we have it. Yet, if we were flowing the high frequency of joy all the time, rather than any lower vibration which joy is not, we would be overflowing in such a profusion of prosperity, affluence, and success—not to mention sublime happiness, perfect health and well-being—that none of this would matter.

So here's the scoop on this state we call normal, which for about 99 percent of the time is nothing but negative vibration:

Negative vibration of any kind, of any intensity, from any excuse, means we've cut ourselves off from Life. We're existing, but not Living. Big difference!

Negative vibrations mean we've shut ourselves off from our Source.

Negative vibrations occur when we refuse to allow ourselves to think about what makes us happy.

Negative vibrations come from living with Don't Wants. And that's the only place they come from.

Negative vibrations mean we've slammed the door shut to our toy store. Not one of our heartfelt desires can ever manifest through the slow vibrations of Don't Wants. They are part of a different frequency called "joy," so they stay away from us—way away—until summoned from the higher vibrations of Feel Good.

It's that simple. Our Wants are only in sync with the high vibrations of our Inner Being/Expanded Self, not with our negative vibrations. Because they will bring us pleasure (in whatever degree), the only vibration they match is that of our Original Intent, to be in joy. We cannot be thinking about what we *don't* want and expect to get what we *do* want. That's like trying to mix oil and water; mixing low frequencies with high frequencies will never happen. One will always override the other, depending on which is more dominant at the time. Even feeling moderately concerned (sort of our life story) shuts the door to abundance and well-being which is our God-given birthright.

So basically, we've been defeating our own purpose all along. Thinking it was important to be concerned about everything like the bills, the kids, grandma, the world situation, what we've been doing is generating this constant flow of low frequency energy to withhold most of what we desire for ourselves, for others, and yes, for the world.

Hooray for Negative

Here's another way to look at it: any emotion that's not in the family of joy is plain-old negative, and comes from lack...of something or other.

Think about it. Every negative emotion we've ever had, no matter how meek or well hidden, has come from the lack of what we really wanted. Take blame, for instance. We blame someone or something for giving us what we *don't* want, which is only the lack of whatever it is we *do* want.

We're worried about losing someone or something, so we're fearing the absence of—the lack of—that someone or something.

We're fearful of things "out there," because we lack the feeling of safety.

We justify and rationalize, because we lack someone's approval (including our own!).

We feel depressed, because we don't have something we want, even if it's nothing more than feeling good.

We feel anxious, because we lack the time or resources to produce.

Every negative feeling in the dictionary comes from lack. And thank goodness for that!

Say what?

Yes, I know, that sounds crazy. But how can you identify what you DO want unless you first know what you DON'T want? Can't be done. Only from a Don't Want can you know a Want, which means that every crummy experience, every ugly event, every unhappy moment, and every minor concern is the opportunity of a lifetime.

A Don't Want is a call to wake up, a call to come out of hiding, switch gears, and pull in real Life. So bless 'em all, every negative emotion you ever had or are having, no matter how abhorrent or commonplace. They're the most valuable assets you have, your springboards to well-being.

Granted, it's going to take a little getting used to the idea of cheering for something like stress. But hey, if you've got it (and who doesn't?) and can admit it and feel it, you've just taken the first and biggest step in learning to be a deliberate creator:

Step One: Identify what you DON'T WANT.

Flavor Doesn't Matter

There are two kinds of Don't Wants; Universal and Personal, with Universal being the most common and the easiest to spot.

Universal Don't Wants are world-wide dislikes, things no one on the planet wants any part of, such as empty bank accounts, sickness, poor relationships, unfulfilling jobs, misshapen bodies, low self-esteem, leaky roofs, broken-down cars, being robbed, being assaulted, being in a terrible accident, even global warming. That's enough for openers.

Personal Don't Wants are simply the mildly unpleasant things of life that bother only us, not always others; things we personally would prefer to avoid such as speaking up at a meeting, killing spiders, sewing holes in Junior's socks, or long-lasting jury duties.

These happen less often than Universal Don't Wants because we don't expect them to happen that much, so they don't.

Let's say, for example, you're really angry at your boss (a personal Don't Want). On the way home you stop at the market, and sure enough, with the way you're vibrating, you get into the line with the snarly babe at the checkout counter. Some people couldn't care less, but today it gets your goat.

You keep on stewing about her on the way home—for well over sixteen seconds—to the point where you've started the thoughts running, the feelings going, and the vibrations moving.

You gripe about her over dinner for a lot more than sixteen seconds, doing a really good job of making that Don't Want vibration a part of you. You talk about her at work (great coffee room material) and tell your best friend the saga at lunch. Now is when you'd better duck, because the energy you've tossed out with such a specific focus on it has grown into a boomerang, and you can bet it's headed back your way.

The next night, out of spite, you decide to go to the store's competitor. You do your shopping, go to the checkout counter, and guess what? You bet! There's another cold-blooded checkout person in your face, magnetized right into your experience by all your attention to the very thing you wanted to avoid. You may be surprised, but you asked for it! You get what you vibrate; there is no other rule of life.

My friend Skip, a connoisseur of fine foods and restaurants, loves surprising his wife, Muriel, with fun, new places to eat. He had me in stitches recently (Skip's also a student of deliberate creating) as he unfolded his story of their trip to a colorful, intimate little place overlooking the water. It had the works: candlelight, a roving violin, even black-tied waiters.

They got settled in, ordered their wine, and as they were savoring the sights of the waterfront, a fight started in back of them. Just muffled noises at first, the voices grew louder and louder until every word of this lover's spat was right in the middle of their cozy setting.

Skip and Muriel tried, without success, to ignore the fracas. It got so bad, so fast, that they both forgot about what was happening to them vibrationally. Although they didn't leave, with their energy merging so swiftly and surely with the couple's vibrations, they would have been better off if they had.

Skip started growling. He asked the maitre d' to please get the couple quieted down. That didn't work. He bristled through the rest of dinner and grumbled about it on the way home. By the time they went to bed, both of them were grousing about it. But it didn't stop there.

For the next three dinners out, Skip and Muriel had—in this order—a bickering couple close by, a crying youngster, and a noisy drunk.

Finally they got it. They had been so deeply focused on what they didn't want, and were flowing so much energy to it, the Law of Attraction was working overtime to pull comparable vibrational circumstances right into their experience. Without paying any attention to how they were feeling, they had allowed a little Don't Want (no ruckus during dinner) to turn into a war.

Personal Don't Wants are usually not that serious, at least not at first. They come from our innate desire to experience the niceties of life, while Universal Don't Wants are deeply rooted and most often fueled from long-standing human fears and insecurities.

But it doesn't matter a diddly damn if a Don't Want is Universal or Personal, intense or mild, constant or passing. The point is to catch it, see it, feel it, or whatever else it takes to identify it...*and change it.*

Which means changing feelings from a Feel Bad to a Feel Good. Fast.

Watch It

The trick to flying up into the wonderful world of Feel Good requires nothing more than starting to think about Wants instead of Don't Wants.

Because Wants and Don't Wants are so easily mistaken for each other, with the usual winner being the Don't Want, here's where we need to use a little caution.

Take for instance the thought, "I don't want to get the flu." While what you're saying is that you *want* to be well, where is your focus? It's smack on what you don't want, so that's how you're vibrating. By the Law of Attraction, if you're giving your attention to it, you're vibrating it and breathing life into it—in this case, the flu.

Or take something like, "I don't want to drive this old car anymore." Okay, you *want* a new car, but your focus is on the old car. Not only are you vibrating in harmony with your Don't Want (to drive your old car), which is keeping your Want of a new car away, but that focus is likely to start all sorts of things happening to your poor old car that aren't going to be too pleasant. And if you just happen to be focusing on how much money you don't have to buy a new car or fix the old one, watch how the two come together like bees to honey: the old car breaks down...no money in bank to fix it!

A strong feeling of "I don't want to get a speeding ticket," is a gold-plated vibrational invitation to the cop behind the tree who's drooling, "I'll get that sucker wherever he is." Same negative vibrations, and they come together.

A strong feeling of "I don't want to fail my exam" is a kind of focus you can do without if you want to pass the thing.

A strong feeling of "I don't want my child to get hurt" is a great vibrational prelude to an accident.

"I don't want to be ripped off."

"I don't want to be sick when I'm old."

"I don't want my car to break down."

"I don't want to live like this."

"I don't want so many taxes."

"I don't want to make a mistake."

"I hate war."

All things you want to change, yes, except that your focus has included them in your vibration. Focus on what you Don't Want, and watch it get bigger.

Even more tricky, though, is when we're saying "want," but vibrating "don't want," like so:

"I *want* out of this relationship."

"I *want* a job that pays better."

"I *want* the government out of my life."

"I *want* to get out of debt."

"We *must* stop rain forest destruction."

Where's your focus? In each of those, it's on what you don't want, not on what you do want.

If you're just having a passing thought about a Don't Want, no problem. But if you're giving some passionate attention to something you truly do not want—even when you think it's a Want—it will eventually grow up to smack you.

Make It a Warm Fuzzy

Obviously, none of us are about to stop and scrutinize every thought we have to see if the fool thing is a Want or a Don't Want. We'd be loony in five minutes. No, we don't have to do that. All we have to do is pay attention to how a thought makes us feel.

If what you're saying or thinking makes you feel like sailing to the heavens in sheer delight, you're into a Want (Green Flag).

If it feels as if you just stepped into a soggy dark cloud, you're into a Don't Want (Red Flag). In fact, if it gives you any sort of feeling other than warm fuzzies, you have a Don't Want working. Just rethink, rephrase, refocus, and refeel until you've found a way to snuggle into your warm-fuzzy Want and are vibrating there safe and sound.

Here's a good example: Say to yourself "I want to be happy." Sure, you're saying "want," but you're coming from the *lack* of what you desire. So as you say that, how does it make you feel?. Wonderful? (Doubtful!) Happy?

(Not likely!)

All right, now say, "I want the happiness I have now in my life to expand into ongoing, boundless joy." What's that feel like? A whole lot better, right?

"I want out of debt." No need to ask how that makes you feel. Instead, go for, "I want to use my talents in a way that will be fun, fulfilling, and really profitable. I know I can do that." Or, "I intend to create more time to look into fun, new money-making projects." Or, "I feel alive when I'm being creative." Big difference in feeling from "I want out of…"

But don't get caught up in the words or you'll end up like an inside-out pretzel. Just stay tuned into how you *feeeel* when you say or think something. Then experiment with different statements. When you find one that gives you wonderfully pleasant feelings, you just plugged into your Source power.

And check out how the things you say every day make you feel, like:

"Yeah, I'm sick and tired of that, too."

"Oh, I know, it's awful what's happening."

"Forget it, we don't stand a chance."

"I agree, he's a real problem."

If it doesn't cause you to smile, if it doesn't cause you to feel cushy-warm inside, it's a negative vibration and a Don't Want. If it doesn't feel like a warm fuzzy, either don't say it or change it around.

Here Are Our Choices

Social conscious thinking, meaning that which flows from the masses, is mostly about Don't Wants.

And no fair blaming everybody else for this murky sea of thought we live in. How often have you talked about how dreadful something is? That adds to the sea. Or how many of your friends at work gripe and complain about this, that, or the other thing? That adds to the sea. "Oh hell, another Monday!" That adds to the sea. It's all low-vibrational muck. We exude it; we live in it.

So here are our choices: Either we learn to identify a positive vibration from a negative vibration and take control of our Wants over our Don't Wants, or we stay in this negative sea of garbage to fly as blind as everybody else for the rest of our days. Struggle, discord, conflict, disease, and not a lot of happiness will be our reward.

Harsh words, perhaps, but they come with a simple solution. We become the *generator* of thought rather than receiver! Now we're in a new ball game, no longer living at the whim of others' emotions. We've stopped being the hapless, vulnerable passenger. We're in the driver's seat. Outside forces become irrelevant. The past becomes immaterial. We're finally off the default setting. Our life, forever more, is of our own choosing.

End of Story

My turned-down loan? Well, the minute my underwriter told me the loan had been declined, I put two and two together and realized right off the bat I was into some serious Don't Wants, royally vibrating and flowing the apprehensive energy that had not only whacked my loan, but attracted that whole chain of cute little events in the car.

It didn't take me long to flip the switch from Feel Bad to Feel Good. And I kept at it and at it, even though the loan had already been rejected. Although it looked hopeless, I refused to see it that way any longer and went to work on changing my focus, my feelings, my vibrations, even my clothes when I got home (that's carrying it a bit far).

The next morning, the lender called to tell me they had found a loophole, the loan was approved and would fund in a few days!

Was it luck? No way! It was the deliberate, purposeful change of focus, change of feeling and change of energy flow. I had already gotten what I didn't want, so it wasn't too tough to identify my Want, get into the feeling place of having it, and flow, flow, flow. It's not always that easy to turn a Don't Want around after you've jumped out of the plane without your parachute, but this one worked.

Negative creating has been our bag. We've molded our private worlds from countless barrels of Don't Wants, thus answering the timeless questions of why, why, why. "Why did our lives turn out this way?" "Why aren't we as happy as we'd like to be...could be...might be...ought to be?" "How come we never made it here or climbed up there?"

It's okay! It really is. We've done it perfectly. Without our Don't Wants, we would never have our Wants. Now we just learn to turn 'em around on purpose, instead of by chance.

So if it feels like a yuckie dark cloud surrounding you (or even a mildly damp one), remember you're flowing out negative energy. Just march out of it and make yourself dig up some kind—any kind—of warm fuzzy Feel-Better. Now you're flying Green flags on your way to pulling in your most treasured desires, which is what you came here to do in the first place.

yes yes!
that, that and that!

(Step Two)

Now that we've examined the cheerful information that living from Don't Wants is how we've created the vast majority of our lives, let's get to the business of understanding what Wants really are, and what on earth we do with them once we've uncovered them

Sounds stupid, doesn't it? Everybody knows what they want in life, right?

Wrong! Wants are about the most frightening, misunderstood, neglected element in the entire human race, and I'd lay odds that, for most people, just thinking about them is more terrifying than a dentist's chair without pain killers.

But before we delve into the tantalizing realm of Wants, it's important we understand what it is that gives joy and passion to our lives and makes life worth living. Oddly enough, what gives us happiness is the very thing we think we would like to avoid—contrast: Likes and dislikes, Wants and Don't Wants. As strange as this logic may seem, without contrast, we would probably go insane.

To better illustrate this bizarre concept, come fly with me on an imaginary journey over a fictitious town on a fictitious planet called Sameville.

No Thanks Sameville

There it is, right below us. The area looks just like Earth, has the same terrain, the same-shaped people, same everything. It all seems identical to Earth except for one ghastly condition—everything is gray: the landscape, the buildings, the cars, the animals, the bodies. It's all the same color, even the same shade! The people have no oomph in them, because everything is the same. They have no challenges, no hurdles, no obstacles, *no contrast!*

Notice the inertia of the people? It's boredom, and it's overpowering. Little wonder. No one has to make decisions in Sameville, for all decisions have the same outcome. No mate is different from the next, all jobs have the same level of stimulation, and...have you seen enough? The scene looks about as close to hell as we'd want to get.

Who'd want to live in such a place? What would be the point? Nothing to rise above, nothing to desire, no differences to appreciate, nothing to inspire enthusiasm. Simply a place of incalculable boredom, which is precisely what we came here to Planet Earth to avoid. We came in search of diversity and differences. We came, strangely enough, for the *contrast.*

That's what our third dimensional Planet Earth offers, a cornucopia of alternatives and choices, a training ground to help us determine what kinds of things we don't like, so we can turn around and—thank you very much—create the kinds of things we do like. Like the man said, if the only ice cream ever made was vanilla, life would be pretty dull.

So we have choices; lots and lots of choices offering us not only the opportunities to live and enjoy whatever in this bountiful world we desire, but also to find out just how much torture and deprivation we're willing to put ourselves through before permitting those desires into our lives.

Let's face it, we are unequaled wizards at identifying what displeases us, but not too hot at allowing ourselves to identify what we really, reeeely do want so that we can magnetize those things into our lives for the sheer joy of having them.

Life was meant to be, "Don't like that, *do* like that." Instead it turned out to be "Don't like that, but guess I'm stuck with it." Then we bitch and stew and fuss and gripe about all the stuff we're stuck with, which of course keeps us even more stuck right in the middle of where we don't want to be.

So what do you want? Do you know? Do you dare to dream? Do you dare to desire? Do you dare to let your imagination (the most divine and mighty gift of the human race) run to the winds of fancy? What do you want? What do you dearly, truly want?

The Torture of Wanting

As we back gently into the rather startling awareness that everything in our experience has come from our focus and how we've been feeling, it's probably only natural we should think, "Well, wanting may be okay for others, but I'm not about to start daydreaming like that now. My life's all right, I've gotten by, so why should I open myself up to more disappointments at this point?"

We see all the things we would like to have but don't, all the places we would like to be but aren't, all the ladders we would like to have climbed but didn't. When very little has gone the way we would have deliberately chosen, why start wanting now? It's the old "The more I want, the less I get" scenario, along with the other side of the same coin that says, "Sure I have lots of desires and Wants, but I don't ever expect to get them anyhow."

Sad to say, we've been brainwashed into believing that most Wants are not only self-serving egotistical no-no's, but absurdly impossible.

Do you remember when you were in, say, third or fourth grade? Not only were you old enough then to understand disappointment and how much it hurt, but you were already a seasoned veteran at knowing how to avoid those feelings. You found out early in life that the more you wanted something, the more you experienced the heartache of not having it. You probably just stopped wanting unless, of course, you had an ironclad guarantee that your Want would materialize.

Even before that, as a toddler who relished exploring, you waddled over to the glittering glass vase on the TV set and got screamed at: "No, no, don't touch!" Not once, not hundreds of times, but some *sixty thousand times* (say researchers) in a three-year period you were told, "No, bad, you don't want that!" By the time you reached your fourth birthday, you were thinking twice about wanting much of anything. Wanting equated to "bad."

Nor does it stop after toddler years. "No" to this, "no" to that, "absolutely not" to what seems like just about everything as you're growing up. By the time you get to high school, it's pretty tough to do much real wanting beyond what is socially acceptable, like getting your first car, going to the prom, or working your way through college. God forbid you should want to bum around the world until you think of something else better to do. God forbid you should want to become a millionaire by next year. "Ridiculous! Get your head out of the clouds." So most of us just lay those passions aside as we trudge into the dogmatic Shoulds and Have To's of adulthood.

We have seen the great truth which states: The more we want something outside of society's book of rules, the surer we seem to be of not getting it. We dream, it never happens. We dream a little more, it doesn't come. Pretty soon we bow to the fictitious truth that dreaming of, or wanting anything outside of the norm (and often even within the norm) is just not a fun thing to do. The more we want it, the worse we feel for not getting it.

Finally, with the exception of the littlest dreams, the ones we know are prudent and obtainable, we stop dreaming altogether. And there we stay, in the bleak sanctuary of Sameville, protected by the erroneous belief that if we dream small and nothing happens, we won't be hurt big.

Dear God in heaven, what a way we've chosen to live.

Breaking the Want Barrier

Crashing a lifetime of programmed deprivation can be a bit scary, primarily because it means changing. But crash it we must if we are to become creators by intent instead of creators by accident. And honestly, learning how to want productively (and finding out that it's okay) is not that big of a deal once we learn *how* to want, instead of don't want.

There are three basic kinds of Wants, each with its own purpose in our dream file.

Real Wants

First are the Real Wants that come from the Don't Wants. "I don't want to go to my in-laws for the holidays; instead I want....?" "I don't want to live here any more; instead I want...?"

Those are the easiest. Just turn the page of a Don't Want, and there's your Real Want on the other side.

Negative Wants

Next are Negative Wants, the ones that have to be flipped over before you can step out of them. You can spot them by how you feel, since they never make you feel good until you get your intent refocused.

"I want to be well" has a clear focus on the apparent fact that you're not. That's a Negative Want. "I want to be rich," presents the same difficulty. Both are coming from a place of lack that causes us discomfort by the very fact that we don't have what we're wanting. Negative Wants are always Don't Wants and can be tough to spot unless you tune into your feelings.

If you're overweight and want to be thin, and you say innocently enough, "I want to be thin," that's a Negative Want and will never, ever feel like a warm fuzzy. It's coming from longing, or yearning, or empty wishing, all negative energies. It's coming out of need which is fear; not out of desire which is excitement.

Naturally, you wouldn't be wanting something if you had it, but if your only focus is on the fact that you don't have it, it will never come. It can't, for your focus is on its absence.

If what you want—and the way you are stating it—is *not* making you feel good, it's Negative Wanting and needs to be flipped over to become a positive intent, an excited desire.

Rightful Wants

Finally, the third kind of Wanting I call Rightful Wants for the simple reason that we have a right to our desires, no matter what our religions may say to the contrary, or our parents, or friends, or coworkers. We have a right, by virtue of our existence, to test our creative skills in any manner we choose. We have a right to displace any Don't Want—*any* Don't Want—in our lives with a Want, at any time. And if it pleases us it will probably also please others. If not, well then, so be it.

With Rightful Wants, we finally come out of the closet of "shoulds," and "gotta's" and go for living Life ...our own!

With Rightful Wants, we accept the very real fact that it is not only appropriate and proper, but critical for us to want: anything...anywhere...of any kind...in any amount...in any shape...to any degree...at any time we so desire. Anything! *Anything* on the face of this earth if those things will take our lives off of hold, get us out of Sameville, and start us vibrating closer to the joy channel of our real Selves. This is the only reason we have Wants, to make us feel good when we have them.

Yes, I know, all this may sound callous, uncaring, and grossly self-serving. But, please, bear with me before jumping to conclusions, and you'll see how this outrageous approach to life will also profoundly benefit all who surround and depend on you.

Wanting: The Necessity of Life

I say to you, "Okay, what do you want?" And you say to me, "Oh, that's easy. I want enough money to pay my bills, take care of the kids, have a nice house to live in, a job I like, a loving partner with whom to share it all, and perfect health. I wouldn't mind a new car, either."

Well that's a start, and a good one. But that's all it is, a start! Indeed, to most in this world, having all of those obviously wonderful things would seem like living in heaven! But if we are to unleash that power we call passion where we can finally live closer to the frequency of our Natural Selves in profound joy, we've got to go beyond the obvious...way beyond!

So what else? What else do you want?

Yes, of course, Wants change over the years. You've probably outgrown wanting a pony for your birthday (and then again...?), or a spiffy new hot rod to drag the Main on Saturday night.

Yet still, there is within you an amazing inventory of long-forgotten fantasies. What are they? How long has it been since you dared to savor their tantalizing flavors or partake of their exotic adventures in your daydreams?

What are your smallest, your biggest, your oldest, your newest, your most deeply hidden desires, ambitions, aspirations...the ones that are so far out, so impossible, so unobtainable, that never have you so much as whispered them aloud...to anyone...not even to God? What are they? What have you stopped allowing yourself to want?

This planet is not Sameville! We came here for the contrast. We came here to learn how to manifest our desires. We came to learn discernment and to cultivate this strange art of wanting which equates to manifesting. Instead, we got ourselves caught in the pointless skill of diligently collecting Don't Wants.

We came to learn how to create our desires, fulfill our dreams, prosper, and take this exquisite experience called "being physical" to its zenith.

We came to experience the good with the bad, that we might learn how to choose likes over dislikes.

So have them!

Take your treasured dreams out of that crowded old closet, dust them off with loving care, and give each one a long, hard look.

Forget that they're too far out.

Forget that they're hopeless or too unthinkable.

Forget that someone will think you've lost it.

Forget that you might be called selfish.

Forget those things!

Wanting is not only your right, it is an absolute prerequisite for a happy life.

Oh Yes You *Do* Deserve It

Now here's the big news: you don't have to be worthy of a blasted thing to have your desires.

You don't have to prove, or witness, or demonstrate, or pass a moral test.

You don't have to explain your reasons, or make excuses to your family, to yourself, or to God.

You don't have to be any more worthy, or deserving, or trustworthy, or upstanding than you are now.

You only have to make one decision...just one...and that is to be happy.

But you will never start down that road until you allow your Wants—your dreams, your desires, your hankerings—to come out of the closet, not just peek around the corner of a cracked-open door, but come all the way out!

Like any hidden talent that you've either consciously or unconsciously known was there but didn't feel comfortable bringing out, once you accept the fact that wanting is part of you, and that doing it is really okay, it becomes fun. Joy starts to flow. You begin to vibrate differently, for when you are in joy with Life you cannot vibrate negatively and you cannot *attract* negatively, only positively.

When you are in joy with Life, you cannot feel insecure, ashamed, unworthy, unsafe, guilty, or inferior in any manner, because you aren't vibrating there. You cannot feel lack of any kind. Nor can you attract it.

The only thing you will do as you begin to unlock your Wants is vibrate more joy, more abundance, and more freedom into your experience. Small price to pay for dreaming, wouldn't you say?

And it makes no difference what you choose to dream! Choose your dream because it makes you happy, and you'll vibrate it into your life. Dream the dream of joy, dream the dream of fulfillment, dream the dream of frivolity, but DREAM!

Having desires—wanting—is no more a sin than breathing. Never again think you have to justify your Wants. Just don't! You cannot be justifying, defending, or rationalizing—which is all negative flowing—and remain connected to your core energy.

You need make no excuses to anything, anybody, or any higher or lower authority for your desires. Certainly not to God. To do so is to turn your back on your own higher energy, thus denying your very existence, your divine right to Life. Contrary to common teachings, gaining happiness *is* your hallowed right of birth.

So let yourself go, and dream. You are already creating your life every moment of every day by how you think and vibrate; you might as well create it the way you'd like it to be.

You Still Have Them

One of the best ways to uncover some of those long-hidden Wants is to pretend. Remember, all that's required for you to have it — whatever "it" might be—is wanting it and feeling it, without explanation, excuse, apology, or reason.

The challenge now is to peel the onion down far enough to get past the rigid layers of Shoulds, Shouldn'ts, and No-No's, to the long-forgotten thrill of—and passion for—Life.

Pretend it's Christmas time (this isn't religious, so humor me, no matter what faith you are). You're the Santa Claus at the mall, replete with scratchy beard and pillowed tummy. You're listening to all the wee folk rattle off their long lists of socially acceptable Wants, but after a while you decide to spread around some magic dust so that kids of any age will feel the urge to reveal some of their less socially acceptable Wants.

Up comes a little cutie-pie, about six, who hops up onto your knee. She starts to give you her list: a few special toys as seen on TV, and a couple of the old standbys like a doll and a puppy. That's it. Nothing new.

So you spread your magic dust and out it comes: a big swing in the back yard, a daddy to be around more, a mommy who will take time to play, someone—anyone—who will believe about the pretty angels in the bedroom, and somebody to always make everything all right. Oh, and lots of brothers and sisters, please. Then she jumps down, happy as a lark.

(Do you remember what your secret Wants were at six years of age?)

Next a tall gangling 18-year-old comes up, having fun with the experience and quite willing to go along with the gag.

"All right now, what would you like Santa to bring you?" Once again, even though the teenager is gladly entering into the spirit of this silliness, the list is alarmingly short. "Well, I'll take that new car you got hidden in your sack, Santa. And I wouldn't mind a few thousand dollars in my stocking for play money. And if you just happen to have a hot romance back there in your sleigh, hey, that'd be cool!"

You sprinkle your magic, the 18-year old relaxes, and out comes an amazing list of Rightful Wants having to do with careers, and friends, and success, and fame, and clothes, and living conditions, and family, and yachts, and genuine happiness, "Whatever that is," he mumbles.

(Do you remember what your secret Wants were at 18 years of age, and what dreams got stuffed away so that you could live in "the real world?")

Finally comes the adult, gleefully hopping up on your Santa Clause knee as the kids watch and snicker.

"And what would you like, m'friend," you ask expectantly. You're dismayed to find that this person has the shortest list of anyone so far, as though every hope and dream ever owned just flew to the next galaxy. Oh, there's the new house, and new car, and a flippant crack about winning the lottery, but that's it. Quickly you sprinkle your magic dust. Nothing. You sprinkle more. Still nothing. You empty the bag.

Slowly at first, as if having to be pulled up from the deepest, darkest depths of the ocean, comes a comment about having a pie shop. And another about learning to play the piano. A pause, and then another about taking a horticultural course at the local college. And another about building a unique kind of sailboat. This one's on a roll now. There's another about being able to financially help a friend open a dance school, and another about having an automatic garage door, and another about living in an elegant home overlooking the aqua blue waters of a Caribbean island.

There's no stopping now. Another deep desire pours out about being able to talk with partner about daydreams. And another about opening a summer camp for city kids, and feeling safe in earthquake country, and something about having the confidence to talk in front of a group of people. There's one about improving relations with certain family members, and learning how to be more loving, and on, and on, and on. It took a full bag, but the dam holding back those long-forgotten treasures finally broke.

What dreams have you put aside? Your ambitions, your forgotten goals, even your littlest desires—what are they? *WHAT ARE THEY?*

Step Two: Identify what you DO WANT

Who's on First!

Back in the forties, the adored comedy team of Abbott and Costello had a routine that always brought the house down and ultimately became a classic. It was their "Who's on First?" routine that started something like "Yes, Who's on First."

"Well, if Who's on First, then who's on second?"

"No! Who's not on second, he's on first and What's on second."

And around and around, until everybody was in tears of laughter. To this day I go into stitches whenever I see it replayed on TV.

Well, if you were to take the paradox we're about to get into now, it sounds just as loony as "Who's on First?" Like so:

If I take all my Don't Wants—which make me feel bad—and turn them into Wants—which are supposed to make me feel good—I still end up with something I know I don't have—which sure doesn't make me feel good—and something I'll probably never get anyhow—which makes me feel worse than I did before I started this whole stupid thing!

Ah, 'tis a great predicament, because if you had it, you wouldn't want it.

So the very act of wanting carries with it the rather obvious implication that you surely do not have it, and if you do not have it, how in the Sam Hill can you feel good about it until you get it?

You can't! Not as long as you keep wanting things the old way.

The dilemma comes from our thinking that the burden of acquiring what we want is all on us, that we're the ones who will have to figure out how to get it, how to come up with the money for it, how to arrange for it, how to make it happen. Once we get that far, our next thoughts are usually something like, "Oh hell, that's just not possible," which invariably causes us to stop wanting. Easy resolution, straight from our old programmed way of thinking.

The Key

The key to having whatever your most divine heart desires—bar nothing—is finding a way to feel good about your Want: not wish for it, yearn for it, long for it, sigh for it, or feel discouraged about it, but just feel good about it. (Remember, need is from fear, desire is from excitement. They are at the opposite ends of the vibrational pole.)

So here we are in this quandary. We're wanting, which usually makes us feel bad, because not only do we not have what we want, we haven't the foggiest idea how to get it.

The solution? *Change the feeling!*

When you want something, hold your thoughts on that Want for a few moments until some sort of feeling comes up: any kind, good or bad, Red Flag or Green Flag, doesn't matter. Then tune into that feeling. If you feel low instead of jazzed, disheartened instead of turned on, you're thinking about *not having* instead of *having.* You're thinking about the *lack* of what you want.

On the other hand, if you're feeling even a twinge of excitement, or a nice warm buzz, you're on target.

The whole process of creating on purpose is about getting our thoughts OFF what we don't want, ON what we do want, *and keeping them there.* Once we've gotten that far, our job is to find ways to feel good about those Wants instead of lousy when they're nowhere to be seen and would appear to have no way of showing up.

So the question is, how do we get from down to up every time we think about a Want, because as soon as we're up, we're vibrationally overriding all those downer feelings we get when we're focused on the obvious fact that our Want is nowhere in sight.

Becoming Jazzed

We already know that the trick to turning a Don't Want into a Want is to find ways to feel *splennnndid* about that Want instead of discouraged. And it doesn't matter if it's an old one that's been locked away in your Want closet for ages, or a brand new fresh desire; the process is the same.

So here's how we feel good—in fact terrific—about wanting something we don't have, or we think is impossible to obtain, or don't deserve to have, or could never afford, and is entirely too complicated for a tired brain to figure out anyhow. This is the most important component of the Law of Attraction that is guaranteed to pull in Wants rather than Don't Wants:

Once you know what you want, you must find the FEELING PLACE of having that Want, while at the same time staying out of the feeling place of not having it.

In other words, *feeeel* (get jazzed about) what it would be like to swim (if you don't know how), rather than feeling embarrassed when everyone but you runs into the water.

Feeeel (get jazzed about) yourself in your new job, rather than constantly crabbing about—and feeling trapped in—the one you have now.

Feeeel (get jazzed about) your pride in accomplishment as you approach the platform to receive your well-earned degree, even if you haven't started classes yet.

Feeeel (get jazzed about) what you want your new mate to be like, and how great it will be being together.

Feeeel (get jazzed about) what it will be like owning your own airplane, and the joy and pride of flying friends and family all over the place.

Now you're vibrating in harmony with your greater Self. Your desires are joyously included in your vibrations, magnetizing, growing bigger each time you *feeeel* the reality of them for just sixteen seconds. You've broken out of the negative vibrations of social consciousness to live in—and vibrate in—the only energies that are capable of drawing that Want to you, the higher, hallowed frequencies of Feel Good.

Once in that space, you and your Want are literally pinging together. Instead of flying Red Flags and pinging in harmony with the lack of your desire (which means you'd be pulling in more lack), you're flying Feel Good Green Flags and pinging in harmony with having it, whether "it" even exists yet or not.

As long as you don't spend too much time worrying about why "it" hasn't it shown up yet, that jazzed, stoked, turned-on, high, happy vibration you feel when you think about having it will eventually magnetize it right into your lap.

That's all it takes, good feelings, one of the rather important elements of living that we as a species seem to have forgotten how to embrace as steady diet.

The Whys Have It

To help a Want magnetize in, we need to get our juices running so we can to flow out as much positive, excited energy as possible. One of the best ways to do that is to talk about the "whys" of wanting something. The What defines, but it's the Whys that charge your battery and start the juices running.

It's like asking a guy who's bonkers about eating steaks blood-rare why he likes them that way. He'll tilt his head back, close his eyes and drift off into la-la land as he describes the tastes, savors the juices, caresses the texture, and withers under the heady bouquet. That's big-time feeling and big-time vibrating, all from a single little question: "Why?"

As you think about all the Whys of wanting something, you begin to latch onto it in feeling. You get more turned on, more passionate. And, you're creating a whole lot more sixteen-second intervals to flow highly charged, very magnetic energy to the thing rather than just blurting out, "This is what I want."

So by stating your Whys, you're giving that Want a much-needed jump-start. Like your car with a dead battery, until you energize that battery with a charge, your car is going nowhere. No charge, no go; no oomph to your Want, no magnetism; no magnetism, no get.

Because...Because...Because

In one of my weekend seminar groups, a gal spoke up with, "All right, I understand now that I've been focusing on the lack of my dream, but I can only come up with one Why."

"Okay, what is it you want?"

"I want a summer cottage by the ocean." (No oomph.)

"Why?"

"Because I hate being housebound in the summer."

Ah ha, a major Don't Want. I kept asking why.

"Why don't you want to be housebound in the summer?"

"Because I like the feeling of leisure and relaxation I get from a summer house. And freedom, yes, I like the freedom."

"Good! You're starting to connect; let's keep going. Why do you like the freedom?"

"It makes me feel good...and happy. Oh yes! I remember feeling so happy as a youngster in our summer home. It was a wonderful feeling."

"Now we're getting there. Tell me more; what's your summer home like?

"Well, it's a gray Cape Cod cottage, kind of weather-beaten, but so homey. And it has white trim. Oh, how I love the crispness of that white trim."

"More. Is it close to the water?"

"Oh yes, right on the dunes."

"Why do you want to be close to the water?"

"Oh, because it's so soothing, even in the stormy

weather. It makes me feel real, and alive. I can paint there, and watch the sunsets, and lose myself in the vastness of it all, and well, everything just comes alive in me by the sea."

Yes! Finally this gal was cooking on the front burner! Her juices were running and her vibrational frequencies were becoming higher and higher, magnetically charging up that growing Want-thought with every new thought she fed it. I kept asking why, and she kept telling me because, because, because. And with each because, her frequencies were soaring. This "thing" was now becoming a part of her, incorporated in her vibrations.

Ask yourself over and over why you want something, and keep asking, and keep asking, and keep asking, even when you think you have no more answers. Then pretty soon you'll be in dreamland feeling *mah-vel-ous,* just where you need to be to magnetize this thing in.

Now! Here's where you want to summon your will power to stay in that vibration as long as you can, maybe up to half an hour or even all day. But if it's just a couple of minutes, great, that's enough to get the swirl of energy started. Remember, you need only sixteen seconds to get the same vibrational thoughts clumping into an energy vortex, then another sixteen seconds, and another, and another. If you slip into "Forget it, that's just an impossible dream" in the middle of your upper, simply change vibrational gears, think about something that makes you feel good, get your motors revved up again, and you'll quickly override that Red Flag vibration.

(Don't forget, the universe gives us not what we speak, or what we deserve, or what we're supposedly destined to have. The universe gives us precisely—and only—what we are vibrating in every moment of every day.) Nothing more, nothing less.

Before you know it, the Universe starts responding to your vibrations with little signs here and there, amazing little "coincidences," all the magic pieces necessary to put this thing together. They just keep coming, and coming, and coming until it's all in place, with you right smack in the middle, living your once "impossible" dream.

But you gotta taste it, feel it, smell it, and drool over it before it's going to happen. You gotta talk about it until you can feel yourself living it, and then talk some more until those turned-on feelings, the fundamental element of Step Three, come to you with the utmost ease.

Step Three: Find the feeeling place of your Want.

That Magic Valve

One of the best ways I've heard to describe Feel Good energy is the analogy of a valve, or nozzle, the kind you find on a firehose. We're the valve, and the firehose is what carries the energy flow from our Source, that greater part of us that we're forever connected to.

That stream of nonphysical energy is what we really are, an unfathomable force of joy, abundance, and security. Most of the time we keep ourselves cut off from that full stream of energy. How? With our closed-valve negative energy.

But when we tune in, turn on, and feel good, we open that magic valve to let our high-vibrational flow flood through us. Now we feel alive, up, vibrant, energetic, excited, turned on...all better known as happy.

Like the water pressure in our hose, the energy is always there, but we have to take purposeful, deliberate steps to open that rusty old valve if we want our high frequency Source energy to flow through.

Having an open valve (feeling good) means positive energy is flowing to us, through us and from us, and we're creating on purpose.

Having a closed valve (anything that feeling good isn't) means we're flowing negative energy, resisting our natural flow, and creating by default.

This doesn't mean we have to be flapping around higher than a kite all day long. All we have to do is squeak open our valve even a crack, and we instantly let in a little bit more of that Life-giving flow. If we can find ways to feel just a tiny bit better than before, one little feeling at a time, then we've begun the reversal of a lifetime of negative attraction.

Intending

After you've started to get your Wants out in the open, there's one more step that's helpful here, and that is turning your Wants into Intents. Because the word "want" might still cause some emotional blisters to erupt, you may feel a whole lot better "intending."

Intending is sort of a combination of "I want and I expect." And a good place to start is by intending for *small things* throughout the day. Not only does this provide some valuable practice along with rapid evidence, but it opens up new and much needed energy pathways that have never been opened before. And each new pathway means you're receiving more of that higher flow of Source energy than you were before, so feeling good becomes easier...which opens you to more and higher energy...which...etc., etc.

Daily intending develops these new outlets for the energy to flow through. The more we intend, the more we're using that high-frequency energy which quickly becomes a two-way street; the more we use it, the more of it we're getting. This creates a sort of protective cover around us, like wrapping ourselves in a safety blanket where we have much less chance of being side-swiped by old beliefs that continue to bring us things we don't want.

I make it a point to intend with little things all day long. I intend to arrive at my destination safely. I intend to be on time and feeling great. I intend to find a convenient parking place. I intend to feel good in my clothes. I intend to sign the deal. I intend to keep my bank account at a certain level or beyond. I intend to find joy all throughout the day (not such a little thing). I intend to help my clients feel at ease. And, as long as my valve is open while I'm intending, they always come about.

On the larger issues, if your intent for the day is to feel joy, you wouldn't even be able to find an upsetting show on TV. If your intent is to have your new kitchen installed without a hitch, that's the way it will be unless you close your valve over something. If your intent is to finish the harvest before supper, watch how easily you get it done.

With major, larger Wants, if you will turn every Want into a statement of intent, and allow yourself to feel the power behind it, like *YEEEESSSSSSS!!!!!!!*, you'll be amazed at what transpires.

"I INTEND to move by next year!" means "I haven't a clue how it's going to happen but I know I'll find out, because I'm determined to do it!"

"I INTEND to have a new relationship!"

"I INTEND to learn to line-dance!"

"I INTEND to have a full bank account!"

"I INTEND to find happiness in all that I do!"

"I INTEND to make new friends!"

"I INTEND to find a deeper spiritual connection!"

You must feel the strength when you speak it. Feel the authority, the force of command, the muscle behind the energy leaving you. The completion.

But use with caution. Intending is a dynamic unto itself not to be abused and never to be turned into a mindless habit.

Dare to Want

Whether you call it intending or wanting, take off your shackles and do it!

Dare to want. Dare to dream new dreams. Dare to take your old dreams out of the closet and dust them off.

Give yourself permission to want; in fact, *make* yourself want.

105

Then pick a funky, nonessential little Want and start talking about why you want the thing until you get the hang of clicking into that turned-on feeling. Before you know it, you'll be having physical manifestations on your hands, and I'm here to tell you, when that happens, it's a screamer of the first degree.

Check out what you like or don't like about what you've got in your life right now. Then get over the guilt of wanting and get that Want motor revved up, for wanting brings the passion, passion brings joy, joy brings more wanting, and now you're creating on purpose. You are the inventor and partaker, all in one. (Never mind being the design engineer who has to figure out how something will come together. That's no longer your job.)

Go for material things, of course, but also stake your claim for universal or intangible things such as:

I want joy to radiate through my heart.
I want my whole family to feel joy
I want to know that everything is always okay
I want to have a greater sense of freedom
I want to know I have choices
I intend to see more choices
I intend to trust that all is well with the world
I intend to learn deliberate creating
I intend to learn to become an energy manager
I intend be aware of my resistance
I intend to be aware of my feelings
I intend to enjoy life to the fullest
I intend to have more fun
I intend to lighten up

I intend to have a closer connection with my Source.

The point is to get over the stigma of wanting, and do it. Dare to want whatever in this whole wide world will give you pleasure, for wanting is taking charge. Wanting is creating. Wanting—and manifesting those Wants into reality—is fulfilling your reason for being. And therein lies the true richness of Life.

conditions be damned!

This whole process of deliberate creating is really quite simple, but not always easy. At least, not at first. In fact, I'd be inclined to say it's a bitch. But once you get the hang of how you're focusing and flowing your energy, and see what the all-too-obvious results of that are, it becomes a snap. Well, almost!

Let's do a quick review before diving in deeper, and take a look at how far we've gotten into the Four Steps of Deliberate Creation.

We've reasonably examined Step One:
Identify what you DON'T want.

We've moderately examined Step Two:
Identify what you DO want.

And we've taken a pass at Step Three:
Find the feeling place of your Want.

Now we're getting to the real guts of Step Three, the tough part: learning how to feel good about something we want and don't have.

You know as well as I do that our usual thinking has been along the lines of, "When what's over there comes here, *then* I can be happy," or "When I have the right body, *then* I can feel good about myself." "When I'm making more money, *then* I'll be rid of stress." The old gotta-find-a-way-to-fix-it-so-I-can-be-happy syndrome.

Yet it's been precisely that kind of thinking that has made our lives so difficult. When circumstances have not suited us (which is more times than not), our first reaction has always been to search for physically aggressive remedies to remove it, release it, repair it, correct it. We are, after all, physical beings. "Don't like it? No problem!" Whack, bang, smack: fix it!

But, if whatever it is we're trying to accomplish doesn't get fixed, or it seems too big to change, or too overwhelming to attain in a time frame which suits us, we get all disgruntled and frustrated. And you already know the results of that scenario; in the energy of our disgruntledness and frustration, we're simply attracting a whole lot more of whatever it is we're trying so darn hard to fix.

She Started with "Safe"

My old college friend Liz had lived with her husband for years in a well-to-do area of Arizona, raising two children and working as a volunteer for her favorite humanitarian organizations.

When her husband, Clint, died recently, Liz was faced with some rough decisions. She hadn't worked for three decades, but getting some money coming in was mandatory. The family had moved into a large new home only three years before Clint's death, a home that came with hefty payments but very little equity, so that selling the new place to purchase a smaller one with smaller payments was not an option. The worst part was, Clint had left very little life insurance.

Without warning, Liz found herself between a rock and a hard place. If she sold the house, there wouldn't be enough to buy a smaller one. If she kept it, she was facing payments she couldn't afford. Sure, the kids offered to help, but that would provide her with only temporary relief.

Liz's one talent was her artwork. She was an accomplished watercolor artist and her paintings of the Arizona desert were a delight to behold. She had never sold much commercially except to admiring friends, but now she found herself with the enticing possibility (if not necessity) of becoming a full-time professional artist. Being a gutsy gal, she decided to go for it amidst protests from her offspring that she should find something more traditional, like a sales job with a local department store.

Between what Clint had left her, their small savings, and what she borrowed from the kids, Liz had enough to keep her going for about a year. But every time we talked, it was, "Gosh, I haven't sold anything yet, I don't know if this is going to work or not. I've got to sell something pretty soon or I don't know what I'll do."

Liz was not a student of flowing energy, nor did she care to be. She'd listen politely to my sometimes not-so-gentle suggestions that she stop focusing on her current negative conditions (lack of sales) and start focusing seriously on what she wanted and how that felt to her.

Over and over we talked. Over and over Liz would say, "I don't think I can hold out much longer. I'm getting so nervous I can't even concentrate on my painting. What am I going to do? I'm terrified."

One day I just couldn't hold back any longer. Acting out of good old "tough love" for a dear, dear friend, I started talking low, slow, and very firmly.

"All right, my friend, if you want to sink your own ship, be my guest. I wash my hands. Enjoy your misery, and please don't call again with your problems. You could turn them around in no time if you'd stop belly-aching, so whenever you're ready, give a call. I mean it, no more calls until you're ready to take control."

I felt like a heel, but I wasn't going to become another link in her Chain of Pain.

For three weeks, all was quiet on the Arizona phonewaves. When the call came, I could have cried. "You win, I give up. What do I do?" And she meant it!

First I got her talking about all the things she didn't want. That was easy: lose the house, lose the respect of her friends and children, lose the chance to paint professionally.

Then we started on the Wants, piece by piece. We zeroed in on the house first as that was the most pressing...that, and any other subject relating to money. Liz could speak of nothing else because that's all she'd been thinking about. Her paintings weren't selling, so all the money was going in the wrong direction...out!

"Okay, Liz, the first thing we're going to do is get you feeling good and vibrating differently."

"Feeling good?! You twit! How on earth do you expect me to feel good when I'm about to lose everything

Clint and I ever had? That's why I'm calling you, to figure out how to sell my paintings. If they'd start selling, everything would be okay and I'd feel as good as you want me to feel."

That was precisely the problem. All Liz could see in front of her was the *lack* of what she wanted. The more she looked at all she didn't have, and all that was not coming in, the worse she felt. The worse she felt, the more frantically she'd run around in circles trying to turn it around. The more she ran, the worse she felt, and the worse she felt, the more nothing sold. She was focused completely and perpetually on the grim conditions of the moment, believing them to be the sum total of her reality. Facts were facts. Her attempt at supporting herself through her art was not working. "I've got to face reality," she'd sigh with resignation.

But I kept at it and finally got her turned around to talking about why she wanted to keep the house, which at the time she felt was a preposterously stupid thing to be talking about.

"All right, all right! I want to keep the house so I won't have to move." (That was a Don't Want, but I wasn't about to confuse her with details.)

"And why don't you want to move?"

Suddenly there was a softening as she said, "Well, because Clint and I loved this place so, and it still feels like 'our' place, like Clint is still here with me." (Her resistance to Feel Good energy was softening.) "None of that feeling has gone, and I do so cherish the way it makes me feel...except when I think about having to make the payments."

Bit by bit, we worked more into her love of their home until I heard such a sweet joy coming through. She was feeling good, and then some. Her valve was wide open.

"Liz! Stop! Right this moment I want you to feel what you're saying."

"What do you mean?"

"How does what you're saying make you feel?"

"Well, wonderful, of course! Nurtured, taken care of...my God, safe! Oh yes! It feels so warm and safe!"

"Good! Now hold on to that feeling. Got it?"

"Yes, I've got it."

"Feels good, doesn't it!"

"Sure it does, it feels great."

"All right. From that place of safety, from that place of feeling so good, think about how you'll feel when you're easily making payments on the house. Never mind *how* you're going to do it. Never mind you can't do it right now. Where you're going has nothing to do with where you are now. Nothing! You've got to remember that. This condition you see yourself in doesn't mean a thing. Once and for all, take your focus off of it or you'll never get where you want to be. Got it?

"I think so, but how..."

"Never mind how! Your only job is to find ways to feel good, and to forget about what's staring you in the face. You want to find ways to feel a little better, and a little better, and a little better until you feel pretty good, and when you feel pretty good, in *those* moments think about making those easy payments on your house. Can you do that?"

"Oh, I don't know..."

"Okay, how does being able to make those payments make you feel?"

"Terrific!"

"Of course. Think about the thrill of selling your paintings, not from a place of 'gotta-do-it, gotta-do-it,' but with a 'yeowee, I AM doing it' kind of elation. When you think about it from that perspective, how does that feel?"

There was a long pause, then, "Oh gosh, freer than a bird. Heavenly!"

"Right! That's the feeling! That's what I want you to go to...that feeling...all the time. Liz, take your focus *off* of your current negative conditions. Stop looking at them, stop thinking about them; that only makes you feel worse. You've got to remember that your only job is to feel good. Period! Then let the universe take care of the rest."

Liz felt so wonderful talking about how she and Clint loved the house that she figured she could re-create that feeling fairly easily. At any rate, that's where she began.

It took three months and a phone bill that would kill a cow, but at the end of that third month (which just happened to coincide with the end of the year Liz had originally given herself to make good with her art), not only had Liz sold enough paintings to cushion herself for a while, but she had acquired an enthusiastic agent (or whatever you call them in the art world), she was scheduled for her first local showing, and she had been commissioned with a fair amount of dollars up front to do a small mural in a private office building.

Liz got the message, and is now very careful as to how she flows her energy. In truth, I'm not sure which of us was more elated at the turnaround.

Our Cherished Problems

Liz was just doing what we all do, running around like a chicken with its head cut off as she tried to fix all the circumstances of the moment that scared her. Like a drowning person struggling against the lifeguard, the more frightened and hopeless she felt, the harder she fought with negative energy to find ways to remedy her situation.

She was looking at the mess she was in—her disastrous conditions—finding them not to her liking, and frantically wondering how to change them through "normal" physical means. And the more she tried to fix-fix-fix, the more negative energy she flowed and the worse things got. Everywhere she looked from within the dark hole she thought was her reality, she saw nothing but gloom.

We've all been there. When things get rough, we either brood about it or hastily plot for ways to execute damage control. Fix it, improve it, rectify it; is there one among us who hasn't mused, "If I could just get from here to there, everything would be fine!"

We are fix-it mongers, dutifully trained to respond to whatever conditions are in our face.

But fixing is resisting our natural energy. Fixing is a closed valve. Fixing is whopping negative energy.

The challenge is to take our focus *off* the object of our anxieties or irritations, and find the happier feeling of what we want in its place. In other words, we need to stop fixing, and start feeling good.

Let's say, for instance, your roof is old and needs to be replaced, but you don't have the money to do it right now. However, it's the rainy season, so the problem is somewhat pressing. You're also having major problems with the car, and the IRS is dunning you for back taxes.

You've got a batch of nasty conditions on your hands, none of which are going to make you feel particularly sunny as you think about them. But think about them you do. And think about them. And think about them. So of course they get bigger.

All of those negative conditions, known more endearingly as "problems," are nothing but irksome Don't Wants, but they are so common to us and such a part of our world, we take them for granted as part of life. In fact, we wear them as honored badges of identity, a sort of one-upmanship in the sorry game of who can be the biggest victim. And naturally, the more we stew about them, or brag about them, the bigger they become.

Some negative conditions are serious problems, others simply minor annoyances, yet whatever they may be, they are so prevalent, so all-pervasive that we've made them a way of life. However, negative conditions are nothing more than the result of our own past focus...and feelings...and energy flow. That's all they are. Our negative energy flow was the cause, and the unpleasant conditions are the effect.

There is only one way to stop the messes in our lives from getting worse: *stop focusing on them.* If we can accept—from the depths of our being—that our problems are not caused by our boss, our mate, our raucous kids, the IRS, or the drunk on the freeway, then we have a chance to wipe those problems away in the same way we attracted them: by our energy flow. Only this time, through a significantly different vibration.

I'm not going to pull any punches; this is tricky. Staring at—and responding to—what's in our face is what we do. To change that means we would have to give up our cherished right to have—and agonize over—our precious problems.

Well, fear not. As long as we are physical, we will always be faced with conditions we neither like nor want (otherwise we'd be living in Sameville), so there will always be plenty of problems around for you to focus on if you should want to cut loose on occasion and flood yourself with negative energy (as I frankly enjoy doing from time to time). But our goal now is to change the way we *react* to our unwanted conditions so they cease being the focal point of our lives.

Never, Never Face Reality

Because of our upbringing, and because of attitudes passed down over countless generations, we believe that what we see in the moment, and what we are experiencing in the moment, is the way it has to be until we either find a way to eradicate or accept it. We can see it, we're surely experiencing it, so in our book that makes it reality.

And yet reality—*real* reality—is nothing more than the result of how we've been flowing our energy.

Let's say, for instance, you're living in a body you don't much like. You call that reality, which equates to that which is unchangeable and must be accepted.

Or let's say you're currently living in a declining economy which is affecting your income. You call that reality, a potentially disastrous condition over which you have no control.

"That's life; accept it!"

"That's the way things are."

"You can't fight City Hall."

"Stop knocking your head against a brick wall."

"That's the way of the world."

"Learn to take life on its terms."

"Within every life a little rain must fall."

"Get your head out of the clouds."

"Life isn't fair."

"Wise up and face reality."

Here's the flash: We do not have to face up to or put up with anything. All we have to do is learn to flow our energy differently, for nothing—*nothing*—affects our experience except how we flow our energy. *NOTHING!!!*

With some things in our lives, those that are pleasing to us, our valve is naturally open. Because those conditions gratify us, our positive energy is attracting more positive things.

But as we look at the majority of negative conditions (problems) around us, our valve is slammed shut. Our connection to our Source energy is barely enough to keep us breathing, and we wouldn't know a vibration of

119

joy if it walked up and smacked us in the face. We're annoyed at this, steamed at that, worried about them, wondering how to correct this, complaining about that, afraid of God-knows-what-all, depressed over everything, and vibrating such unceasing currents of negative energy all the time, it's a wonder we ever have any moments of joy at all.

Just because you're living in the "reality" of a jobless market does not mean you can't attract a great job.

Just because houses are not selling does not mean you can't attract a qualified, delighted buyer.

Just because your body is not as strong as others does not mean you can't attract the strength to win the 400 meter race.

Just because you've never worked in that market does not mean you can't attract the ability to be successful at it.

Just because you've never been able to stop smoking does not mean you can't attract the willingness to stop right now.

Just because you've had two divorces does not mean you're doomed to attract another catastrophe.

Whatever mess—or happiness—we are living in this very moment, whether it be as an individual, a family, a nation or a planet, that mess is the sole and direct outcome of how we were feeling—and flowing energy— yesterday, and the day before that, and the years before that. The Law of Attraction doesn't work a little here and a little there. It simply is: for you, for me, for the cosmos. We magnetically attract what we vibrate, and we have created it all, from fender benders to global wars.

So, from this moment on, never, ever accept reality as something to which you must resign yourself. Take your thoughts beyond whatever is in front of your nose that you don't like and put them on what you do like. If you don't, your so-called reality will never change. Granted, some ugly things may be glaring you in the face right now, or threatening you, or looking like a hopeless situation, but they are not set in stone! They must never be reluctantly tolerated.

Unpleasant reality is nothing but an effect caused by negative energy flow. We can either live with those effects and suffer, or circumvent them and have a ball.

Tricks to Switching Focus

As a kid, did you ever jump off a high dive? Do you remember that very first time you climbed up...and up...and up? Each step seemed to take you farther away from safety, but even though you were scared, you kept on going.

Finally came the top of the ladder. You walked tentatively out to the end of the board. Your heart pounded so hard you could barely hear the kids below shouting you on. The water seemed five miles away. You didn't really want to do this thing, while at the same time you did. Something in you knew this was epic, the greatest moment you would ever know, that if you did this, you would never be the same. You jumped. What a rush! You made it. And indeed, your life had changed forever.

The toughest part of ungluing ourselves from the high dive habit of an on-going problem (for that's all problems are...are habits) is forcing ourselves to release our preoccupation with it. Like so:

You don't have to change it;
You just have to stop focusing on it!

Is it tough? Yes! Can it be done? You bet!!! But you have to start someplace, and that someplace is a decision that, somehow, you're going to change your focus. Then comes actually doing it, changing your focus to something more pleasant so you can change your energy. It is impossible to solve a problem in the same frequency in which it was created, so you make a decision that for as long as it's with you, *that problem will no longer be the focal point of your life.* Like having a cut on your finger; you know it's there and yes it hurts when you think about it, but you don't allow it to govern your everyday living. You believe it will heal and go away, and so it does.

Just remember, the most important part to changing an unwanted condition is simply: *you don't have to change it; you just have to stop thinking about it!* All it takes is that willingness to jump.

Trick #1. Switch focus. Now!

The moment you recognize you're focusing on the condition with your worry-motor running (or ticked-off motor, or blame motor, etc.), find something else, *anything* else to think about that will get you to feeling even a tiny bit better than you do at present. And find it right now!

Switch your thoughts to your mate (if you've got a great relationship), your home, a song, your doggie, your new sweatshirt, a chocolate sundae, making love, your upcoming vacation, your last vacation, a special restaurant, your youngster asleep. ANY-thing!!! Make yourself do this, staying there until you can feel your mood begin to change—which means your energy has changed—no matter how slight.

Once you make the feeling switch, then start talking—out loud—about what it is you want (that's "want," not "don't want") in place of your unwanted condition. By doing that, your focus is now off of the condition, your Intent motor is running in its place, and you've gotten your valve open enough to begin the turn-around. And for heaven's sake, never mind that your Replacement Want may seem impossible. Just get into it and forget the "how to's."

If you can't get into your Want/Intent feeling mode, never mind. Just stay in the feeling of some pleasant new focus for as long as you can. The longer (and more often) you can stay in that higher frequency, the quicker your unwanted condition will begin to dissipate. Conversely, the more you retain your focus on whatever has been bothering you, the longer it will stay around.

Trick #2. Tender-talk it out. Now!

When you just can't seem to get your focus off the condition, start some soothing talking to yourself, out loud, much like a loving mom or dad might comfort a little one. Tell yourself all the comforting things a youngster would want to hear: that it's going to be okay, that things are in the process of changing, that you've always been safe and always will be, that you have nothing to fear.

Keep talking warmly for as long as it takes you to feel that subtle little switch happen, and you can feel your resistance to the higher energies backing down. You are relaxing into well-being, your resistance to that Life-giving Source energy is lessening, and you're quieting down. Stay there as long as you can, with your focus *off* the disturbing condition.

Trick #3. Tough-talk it out. Now!

This is tough-love kind of talk...out loud...to yourself, one on one. But here's the trick: you need to get *tough,* not *down* on yourself. Don't you ever, ever, ever get down on yourself when you find you're focusing on an unwanted condition.

What you're after here is stern, horse-sense reasoning where you firmly point out to yourself what will transpire if you continue to focus on—and stew over—the condition. Then you tell yourself quite matter-of-factly what will happen when you remove your focus and change your vibration.

"Now look, Charlie, you got yourself into this mess, and you are going to find a way to get yourself out. But if you're going to stay in this mood and stew about it all day long, you know the situation is going to get worse. So get off your pity pot and find some dumb thing to feel good about. Hell yes, I know you don't feel like feeling good right now, but..."

Who cares if you believe it or not? Fake it until you feel the switch in feeling take place, that subtle shift in your energy.

This is an approach of hard logic. While I use it regularly and it always makes me feel better, I find I usually have to jump from this back into one of the other tricks to get more of that quieted-down Feel Good motor running full steam. But that's just me. Whatever it takes for you, go for it!

Trick #4. Do something fun. Now!

Get physical! Go for a walk, polish your car, brush your cat, buy a new suit, bake a cake, play poker, trim your flowers, go to a movie, whatever turns you on that will take your stuck focus off the condition and soften your resistance to flowing that higher energy. Once you feel the shift happen, start talking out loud, gently at first, about what you want in place of the unwanted condition.

With any of these tricks, keep in mind that old expression, "Fake it 'til you make it." You switch focus, you talk warmly, you talk tough, you go for fun, you pretend, but the point is, you do it the *moment* you realize your attention is on the unwanted condition, and you stay there until you feel your feelings flip over. They will!

Conditions Don't Mean a Thing

Once you've taken your focus off the condition and started to get that rusty valve cracked open, you're ready to really crank up your Want and get excited about it.

The shift in focus is: *Away from the unpleasant Now, onto the pleasant Want. Away from the unpleasant Now, onto the pleasant Want.*

If all you can muster at first is just a scrap of Feel Good about your Want, then fine. When you get to having your valve open 20 percent of the time from focusing on your Want, then celebrate! You are headed in the right direction which sure beats vibrating 100 percent of the time about a lousy "what is." Slowly by slowly (as my Hungarian friend used to say), that big chunk of energy that created the condition in the first place is being displaced and replaced by open valve Source energy vibrations.

Pretty soon you'll be able to vibrate at somewhere around at fifty-fifty: 50 percent on the condition and 50 percent on something more pleasant. Now you're truly beginning to take control of your life; sprinklings of your desired changes will start popping up everywhere.

Ah, but the real fun comes when you get to the point of switching energies at the drop of a hat the instant you realize you're tuned to negative. Now you've jumped up to sixty-forty (60 percent with higher frequencies, 40 percent on normal), and finally up to seventy-thirty, or even eighty-twenty. At this point, right before your eyes, you'll watch new events, new people, new circumstances pour into your life as if by magic, one right after the other, to create the new occurrences you so deeply desire. Not too bad for simply feeling good.

Just remember, however fast your Want comes is directly related to how fast (and how permanently) you can switch your focus OFF what is keeping you in a negative vibration, and ON where you want to go. No matter how dire your condition may seem at the moment, it is not permanently glued to you. You just have to decide what you want in place of your problem, then provide the Feel Good frequency that will give it birth.

And please! Don't beat up on yourself if you've got a barrelful of problems, and don't try to tackle them all at once by attempting to project an assortment of unbelievable Wants. We all got ourselves into our various messes, and with some serious practice at taking control of our energy flow, we can all get ourselves out of them. Guaranteed!

Insist to yourself that you will do whatever you can to find—and maintain—*any amount* of Feel Good energy. And remember, the only power present conditions have over any of us is the power we give them. That's when we feel trapped, and quite frankly, we are.

But no circumstances are beyond our control. What's going on in your world at this very moment doesn't mean a thing. It is only a result, that's all it is. No matter how unyielding conditions appear to be, you can always flow Feel Good—even Feel *Better*—energy around them to change them. If you can know that in the deepest part of your being, the rest of this deliberate creation business will be a breeze.

The "Hi Ho Silver" Syndrome

It's taken me longer than I care to think about to own up to the realization that it's not what I do-do-do that makes a difference in my life, but how I'm flowing my energy. I had always been a deep believer in action being the magic word, that nothing would come to me without great effort and exertion.

The truth is that whatever it is we're wanting to fix, all the desperate things we think about doing will have precious little effect on influencing our experience. Nor does it matter *how* we do what we do, or how much, or how often, since most of our doing is initiated out of negative, flap-around energy rather than inspired, breeze-along activity.

Give us a situation we don't like, and, depending on our nature, we do one of two things: we throw up our hands in frustrated resignation, bowing down to accept our fate, or we leap on our big white horse, as the Lone Ranger used to do, and gallop blindfolded (rather than masked) down the trail bellowing "Hi Ho Silver, Awayyyyyy" to frantically search for some heroic action to overcome the dastardly injustice befallen us. Either way, all we're doing is blowing up bigger what we'd like to blow out of our reality.

So let's take a look at this Action business. I call it Frantic Action, the Hi-Ho Silver syndrome, the need to do-do-do in order to fix-fix-fix. It's any type of activity we take with a closed valve.

Most of the world will agree that it's only through "doing" that all things happen. Give us a problem, and we Hi Ho Silver into Frantic Action, looking for ways to sell more, earn more, accomplish more to fix it, fix it, fix it. Yet deliberate creating is about flowing energy to attract, not about trying to push rivers upstream, which is Hi Ho Silvering.

Hi Ho Silvering never works. You just can't muscle into anyone else's world unless you've been vibrationally invited, any more than anyone can intrude on your world unless you've sent out the vibrational invitation. You can not bulldoze something into place and get the results you truly want, no matter how hard you push and shove.

Does this mean we stop doing? Of course not. We just substitute inspired doing for wasted doing by stopping our constant knee-jerk responses to everything. Then, with our focus held enthusiastically on what we prefer in life, the right moves to make come to us from a place of open valve inspiration. Action becomes a joy instead of a "have to." Ideas abound. We open to the Creative Life Force and find ourselves being led step by step, easily and flawlessly, to wherever it is we wish to go.

The miracle has happened. We are no longer responders; we have become deliberate creators.

Bless 'em All

Let's face it, we're always going to have contrast, meaning things we don't like. That's what we signed up for, and frankly, that's what we most enjoy.

But whether it's Godzilla coming around the corner or a flea bite, no matter how bad or irksome the conditions may appear, they deserve no more of our attention than enough to warn us how we're flowing our energy. That's all! They are not the end of the line.

When a feeling-alarm rings in response to a condition, and you get that knee-jerk response to Hi Ho Silver into Frantic Action, just cool down and relax. That changes the thought, which changes the feeling, which changes the vibration and allows the universe and your Expanded Self to take over.

And so, contrary to popular belief, you do *not* have to get all your ducks in a row before allowing yourself to feel good. The only thing you have to do in regards to any condition is to stop looking at the fool thing, stop responding, and find a way to feel better.

Habits of a lifetime—and eons of inherited genes—die hard. Just do your best to remember that whatever you're currently living is only the result of past energy flow.

Then take a quiet step back from the immediacy of the situation to catch a glimpse of that broader view.

Remember that "needing" something to change will always flow negative energy and hold it to you. Finding a way to become excited about what it will be changing into will flow positive energy and get the desired revisions started.

Stop being uptight over anything. Instead, tell yourself in all gentleness that however unpleasant the conditions may seem to you now, they are not going to control you, and that yes, you absolutely can find a way to open your valve in spite of what's happening. And you will!

Then your answers will come, opportunities will come, and you'll soon find more ways to alter your situation than you can imagine.

So bless the rotten conditions if you can, for without them you could not possibly know what you don't want. Cast your gaze to what *can be* rather than *what is,* and dive into all the wonderful feelings—not longings— of how fantastic it will be when you're there. Then, what is there, comes here.

ye gads, I'm feeling!

(Step Three)

Wonder, preciousness, appreciation, gratitude, excitement, reverence, awe. Can you pull up those different feelings any time you want? Can you turn on "wonder" at the drop of a hat, or "excitement" (and I don't mean sex)? Or how about "reverence?" Can you look at anything—even a rock—and instantly make yourself feel a warm sensation of respect toward that inanimate object?

"Turning on" has usually meant getting ready to jump somebody's bones, but that's not what we're talking about here. Our new kind of turning on is a conscious, intentional flipping of our inner switch to a higher frequency to get us vibrating at a faster speed, like *right now!*...any time we remember to do it...every time we remember to do it...all the time...as often as possible...every hour on the hour...or every time you pass a red car, stray dog, or mom and baby. Whenever!

I'm not kidding. If we don't learn how to get our frequencies up there and outta here, we don't stand a bloody chance in hell of becoming deliberate creators. Which means, unhappily, that we will forever remain creators by default. Which means...victims.

Since "Changing Frequencies 101" was never an offered course in school, it becomes a skill we have to learn on our own. But with a few more tricks of the trade under our belts, it can happen easily.

Whoosh!

I first started fiddling around with energy flow about a year before finding the teachings on the Law of Attraction. I didn't have the foggiest idea what I was doing, but it was fun and passed the time as I was driving.

The home refinance market was in full swing, and as a mortgage broker I was right in the middle of it with my own one-person business which I ran from my home. So as requests came in from folks to refinance their houses, I'd go to them rather than the usual routine of having them come to me. It was fun that way. I got out of the house, did errands at the same time, and saw parts of my town I never knew existed.

To pass the time as I was driving around to appointments, I started playing with my energy. I already knew how to switch rapidly into an intense Feel Good mode, a kicky little thing to do I called "running my energy." I'd just inflate a vigorous feeling of "up," and in almost no time my body was buzzing in response to the altered frequency. I also knew if I folded a desire into those high feelings (think about it while I was up), it would stand a good chance of coming about. But that's all I knew! Frequencies, vibrations, negative/positive energy flow, the Law of Attraction—I had only a casual understanding of these things.

The more I fooled around with running my energy, the more I was beginning to see this rather intriguing phenomenon that would occur just as I started to feel high, or buzz, as I called it. Right in the pit of my stomach, that place where you lose your breath when you're socked, there was this *WHOOSH!* feeling as if I was zooming down a roller coaster at breakneck speed. Sometimes it lasted for only a split second, but other times, if I concentrated with extreme care, I could prolong it for several minutes.

Then I realized this *WHOOSH!* was the same kind of *YIPES!* feeling you get if you have to swerve abruptly to avoid hitting another car. Or the kind I felt many years ago at the precise moment my boss told me I was fired. *WHOOSH!*, right in the pit of my stomach.

At first I didn't know what to make of it or how to link it all together. Here were vastly different situations eliciting a broad spectrum of equally powerful reactions, yet they all seemed to end up physically in the same place: my gut. Then it dawned on me. Our emotions register first in our adrenal glands which is why, when we're startled or frighten, we experience that rush in the pit of our stomach, or solar plexus, where the adrenals are located.

When fear hits us, the adrenals are socked with a sudden burst of electromagnetic energy causing the immediate release of adrenal secretion which we experience as *WHOOSH!* So why wouldn't the adrenals respond in the same manner to an intense energy manufactured from joy? Energy is energy, after all, no matter what has moved it around. Whether we feel a rush of extreme panic, or a rush of sublime joy, the energy floods through the solar plexus, stimulating our adrenals, and registering as a highly noticeable, physical sensation: *WHOOSH!*

I was thoroughly intrigued and started to experiment even more. Sure enough, I found I could control how intense my Feel Good vibrations were by how much *WHOOSH!* I had in the pit of my stomach, and vice versa. I could control the intensity and duration of *WHOOSH!* by however much Feel Good vibration I could generate.

It was fantastic! Not much *WHOOSH!* meant not much Feel Good, and not much intensity, so not much change vibrationally from where I had been.

But a big *WHOOSH!* or rush in my solar plexus meant I was really turned on vibrationally to some kind of elevated feeling: excitement, delight, deep appreciation, or whatever. It meant I was flying high without chemicals, and it proved itself every time. The rush never came without my turning on some form of joy. And I never, ever had the rush, or buzz, as long as I was just flat-lining, which is feeling neither good nor bad, but just plotzing along.

I was so excited with all of this, I thought I had discovered the secret of life! Perhaps I had, but only in part. I still didn't know about directing the energy, or about focusing on Wants or Don't Wants. All I knew then was that the more I pushed a Feel Good into a bodily buzz, the more I was attracting my desires. It was a great start, but oh brother, how I wish I'd known "the rest of the story" (as commentator Paul Harvey would say).

In the beginning, I was like Mickey Mouse in the Disney movie *Fantasia,* playing with his boss's magic hat without knowing its powers. I was getting so good at manufacturing up-feelings into a *WHOOSH!,* I could turn it on in an wink, even while listening to tasteless news casts about somebody's sweet grandmother being raped. *WHOOSH!* would come that feeling in my stomach as I turned on the joy, followed in moments by a sort of soft bubbly feeling, or buzzing, all over my body.

The more I buzzed, the more business I'd get, so I'd buzz even more. It was magic. The money was flowing in so fast, I actually stopped counting. Running my energy became such a routine pastime, I could almost forecast how much business would come in by the intensity and frequency of my buzzing.

While I was correct in my understanding that the high frequencies I was originating were magnetizing my desires, I mistakenly thought that was all there was to it. "No problem, just get my frequencies up there, run my energy, and the world is my oyster."

Not quite! What I didn't know then was that even the slightest shift of my focus to anything that was unpleasant would not only pull in the undesired consequences of that negative focus, but would instantly cast a barrier between me and incoming goodies, including money! That little lesson was soon to come.

For several months, though, there was not a negative condition anywhere for me to observe. "What was" was terrific! Everywhere I turned, it was as if it were my time. There was a ripe and ready market which I knew I could tap with ease. The little flyers I inserted into the newspaper were so effective, my phone would ring with loan appointments for weeks afterward. No matter where I looked, things were extraordinarily positive, and of course, so were my vibrations. My energy level was off the charts, my social life was thriving, and my ancient wardrobe sprouted anew from carefree shopping sprees, all while my business boomed. And before the year was out, I had even launched a new enterprise totally separate from the mortgage business. I just kept unconsciously observing the good stuff all around me, running my energy and pulling in more. How good could it get!?

Then things started to go haywire. The market changed and so did my focus along with it. As interest rates began to rise, business began to dry up. Now all my attention was going to, "No, no, don't let the rates go up. Don't let the market dry up. Don't let this gravy train crash." If someone had said to me then that "what is" is only the platform from which you launch your next creation, I would have punched their lights out. I was really, really worried, so of course the problem kept getting worse.

Because I had been so preoccupied with the bad turn of events, I had long since stopped buzzing. Instead, I had shifted my focus completely to what I didn't want (the market to get any worse) rather than to what I could have so easily created (lots of business in spite of the market). But I didn't know that. The worse the market got, the worse I felt. And the worse I felt, the worse my business got. Instead of writing a new script and finding the happy-feeling place of the way I wanted it to be, my fear was pulling in more fear. Trouble was glaring me in the face in major proportions.

136

I had spent all my funds on the new enterprise, the market was in the pits, there were no new loans coming in, I still had debts to pay from launching the new corporation, and...need I say more? The conditions I was focusing on were a long, long way from my liking, and the growing fear behind that focus was making matters meaner than all get out.

I borrowed money to live on. I flew into every kind of Frantic Action I could think of, hired a salesperson who was into more lack than I was (naturally; that was all I could attract), sent flyers farther out into neighboring towns, and generally thrashed about anxiously for new business. It didn't come. I had plunged headlong into creation by negative focus, centering 100 percent of my attention on everything I did not want. I had so entrenched those Don't Wants into my vibrations and made them such a dominant part of me, I was pulling in more and more nasty stuff by the truckload. It was not a good time.

Thinking I still had the secret, I tried to start buzzing again. Good luck! With such impassioned negative focus on all the gloomy stuff around me, I couldn't have turned on if my life depended on it (which at that point, it damn near did). My poor Expanded Self was probably saying, "Forget it," while taking off for an extended vacation in another universe until I came to my senses. Negative was my dominant vibration, and negative was all I was getting. In spades!

It was somewhere right around that emotional low when a bunch of my all-too-enthusiastic friends began insisting I look into this material they had gotten hold of about the Law of Attraction. I was so down in the dumps, I really didn't care if they had discovered a shipload of authentic Aladdin's Lamps, but to get them off my back so I could be alone in my misery, I gave in.

Five minutes is all it took for me to see why they were so excited. At last, here was "the rest of the story," all the pieces that for so many years I never even knew were missing. I couldn't have been more elated if someone had given me fifty million dollars. Within one day I designed—and dove into—my thirty-day program described in the last chapter.

No, things didn't turn around over night; I was too addicted to looking at all the uglies. The financial turnaround was slow but absolutely steady, and a torrent of ideas was beginning to wash over me about fabulous ways to increase business with ease and fun. What excited me the most, though, was the leg up I knew I had in knowing about energy flow, or running my energy. I already knew how to turn on, how to manufacture the up feelings and hold them for quite a while. I even knew how to con myself into thinking I was feeling good until I truly did.

What I most assuredly had not known was the single most important item in the Law of Attraction which says, "What you focus on, chum, is what you get!" All I had to do was get my focus *off* the down market, *off* my lack of money in the bank, *off* the fact there were still no loans coming in, *off* my debts, take precise aim with my focusing, and sail away into the sunset. Oh, sure!

It took more than a little while, but it finally worked. I became one of the few brokers locally who did not go out of business and continued to make good money in a rotten market. What a joy! And eventually, through persistent attention to my focus, I was able to turn my one-person business into a large and highly successful tri-state enterprise.

Buzzing on Command

The art of feeling good is not exactly something at which we are highly accomplished, so the goal is to learn how to do it on the spot.

Sometimes that switching will take a little (or a lot of) prodding; other times you'll find you can switch over in the blink of an eye. But no matter what it takes, the point is to do it, to switch from down to any notch up from there. How? Let's go back into our special bag of tricks.

There are three basic ways to start feeling good, and we've already talked about two of them. One is to look for, or think about, anything that gives you pleasure. The second is to talk to yourself until you bring about a change of vibration. The third, which we'll explore now, is called "buzzing," which gives you a *RIGHT NOW* change in vibration.

Buzzing is one of the easiest and fastest ways to raise your vibrations. Naturally, different occasions call for different techniques. Sometimes one approach will do the trick, sometimes two or three methods are required to drag us out of our addiction to negative emotion. Buzzing is just one way, but it's a technique I've found to be such pure dynamite, I use it almost every day of my life, if only for a moment or two.

One of the reasons learning to buzz is so easy is that there's a jump-start you can use to get it going. What you're reaching for here is a feeling that emanates from the very depths of your being. Once that's activated—a sensation you can achieve in less than a second—your whole body has switched gears to vibrate on a much higher frequency. Your valve is wide open, the Creative Life Force you were attached to by only a thread—just to keep you functioning—is now flooding through you. You are in absolute alignment with your Inner Being/Expanded Self...*and*...you can feel the sensation right smack in the pit of your stomach!

That's what makes buzzing so much fun. Through emotion, you're creating an undeniable physical sensation to use as an indicator of the vibrational change in your body. The whole process is nothing more than a quick one-two, and BINGO! You have turned on.

Jump-Starting

Since we're sort of dead batteries until we get charged, I found the best way to get a buzz started was by doing something physical that would jump-start me into a nice feeling. So, lacking cables, I used a smile!

That's right, a meaningful little smile, the kind that feels like butter melting on a hot roll; the kind of smile you couldn't help but break into at the sight of newborn kittens tumbling all over each other, or a baby giggling just for the sake of giggling. Not a phony grin, but a loving, tender smile as if a youngster had just brought you their most cherished treasure. It's a smile on the outside, yes, but it originates from a rich, caring feeling on the inside.

As you take that feeling and pull it up from the inside, you'll feel yourself smiling from the deepest point of your being. Now you're at what I call the Gentle Inner Smile, a warm, lovely sensation that feels like a soft buzz or a delicate whirling. Maybe even a little tingling here or there.

Now please! Don't go looking for exploding missiles here. The feeling is going to be very, very subtle at first. You're not waiting for a tornado to slam you around, just a delicate—but noticeable—shift in your energy. That shift will always feel like it's coming from inside you, sometimes from behind your ears, sometimes from your heart, sometimes from your solar plexus, sometimes from the top of your head, sometimes from all over you. If you don't feel it right off the bat, stay loose and don't worry. Just state your desire to the universe (to feel the buzz) as a Want or Intent, and I promise it will come.

So, in something like one or two seconds, you've gotten a buzz going with the Gentle Inner Smile (believe me, you'll know it when you have it), and radically changed your energy. It's an instant Feel Good, and an instant raise in frequency jump-started with a warm smile on the outside to that smooth Gentle Inner Smile on the inside.

Next, the Replacement Feeling

The high frequency feeling of the Gentle Inner Smile is fine but hard to hold onto or intensify unless there's some other more familiar feeling to replace it. So you pick some pleasant feeling like appreciation, gratitude, wonder, etc., and hold onto that as your predominant vibration, like so:

1) You jump-start with a facial smile as warm and tender as possible.

2) Right away, and with your physical smile still going, you reach down inside and pump up the tender feeling coming from that smile until it becomes the melted butter, the warm fuzzy of your Gentle Inner Smile, and you can feel a soft little buzz somewhere, no matter how slight.

3) Once you have got the Gentle Inner Smile going, you replace that warm fuzzy with a special flavor of your own choice such as affection, or enthusiasm, or just plain old being tickled pink (one of my favorites.) Pick whatever up feeling is easiest for you to manufacture at will, and hold it there for as long as you can.

4) (Optional!) If you want to, this is a good time in this high energy to fold in a specific Want/Intent, but don't do that until you've gotten used to experiencing the overlay emotion (#3) for a period of time.

That's all there is to it; you're off and running. You've jump-started with a Gentle Inner Smile to get your motor running. Then you've given it the necessary gas to keep it going by overlaying, or replacing, the jump-start with your choice of an elevated emotion.

Let's say you picked Tenderness as your replacement feeling. All right, once you've got your Gentle Inner Smile going, you simply conjure up whatever it takes to get the feeling of Tenderness running. Maybe that's how it feels to rub a glorious rose up against your cheek, or gently caress a loved one, or painstakingly tend to a wounded animal. You want to intensify that feeling as much as you can until you can feel the physical shift of energy in your body, no matter how subtle. What you're experiencing is simply energy in motion made more conspicuous by your switch in frequencies.

At first you may notice the energy *WHOOSHING* in your solar plexus, like that sinking feeling you get in a dive on the roller coaster. The feeling may radiate from your solar plexus up the back of your neck to your head, and you may feel little tingling sensations all over your skull. After a while you may feel it running simultaneously to your head and down to your groin. In fact, you might even feel a slight sexual arousal. Not to worry, it only lasts a moment, but it is proof positive that your energy has finally cut loose and is starting to flux and move around.

The more you practice this, the sooner you'll be able to turn on at will and cause the energies to increase, decrease, or simply remain steady for a length time. I've pumped it up in the car, or the shower, or even the supermarket to such a lengthy time that I've felt not quite of this world (not too smart for the car). But the point is, you absolutely can learn to manipulate your own energy, and that's when the fun really starts.

If you ever want verification that you are opening your valve and initiating high-frequency energy flow about you, just get out the Woo-Woo wands described in the Appendix and go for the Gentle Inner Smile. That's all you'll need to do, then watch your wands go bananas in response to your change of energy.

Positive (Yuck) Aspects

What all this is about is feeling good, since nothing is more important. Nothing! Nothing is more important than feeling good, and it doesn't matter beans how you do it. If standing on your head in Times Square will do it, terrific. If smelling newly cut wood will do it, grand. Anything it takes to get you to that place of feeling better than when you started. You know when you're there; you can't miss it. Whether it's just a decision to feel good in the moment (or even to feel just a little better), or you're orchestrating a new kind of Feel Good around a particular Want, you can usually find dozens of different oddball ways to turn on...if you really want to.

But there's one way I reserve for "when all else fails," because I seem to always resent having to get into it. That last resort for me is finding something positive about whatever irksome thing it was that closed my valve in the first place.

Let's say, for instance, you're stuck in traffic because of an accident, and you allow yourself to get really ticked off. We'll take it as a given that under the circumstances of your closed valve, not only is the traffic not going to improve in a hurry, but all that negative energy is, at that very moment, affecting every other aspect of your life.

Your job is to get that valve open any way you can. But let's say you've "tried" (a word to take out of your vocabulary) and nothing has worked—not music, not buzzing, not talking to yourself. Well, when all else fails, there's only one alternative left. Look for anything within the situation, or in your immediate surroundings, to appreciate or feel good about.

Maybe just the fact that your car is operational, or you don't have to go to the john, or the empathy you're feeling for the other poor slobs on the road who are just as teed off as you are, or your appreciation for the medical response team. Find something...anything! Start talking to yourself about it, fake it, con yourself, and pretty soon you'll feel that subtle little click into Feel Good energy (or at least into a Feel *Better*), and your valve will slowly open. (Because a hundred other drivers are flowing irate energy all around you, the traffic jam might not change for a while, but at least you won't be screwing up other areas of your life by flowing such garbage out.)

Now frankly, when I'm in a crappy mood, there's nothing I enjoy more than staying there. I still love to bitch and stew because it feels so good. The sad part is though, I also know every time I do that, my whole world is being negatively affected, not to mention I'm attracting more of whatever it is I'm bitching about. I'm just not willing to let that happen—much—anymore.

So begrudgingly, I'll find some stupid, dumb, meaningless, insignificant thing about whatever it is I'm mad at that I might—possibly—begin to consider as a positive aspect of this situation or individual; something I might—just possibly—be able to appreciate. Then, looking very much like a defiant brat who has just been scolded, I'll think of some way to begin talking to myself (almost always with a pout) to pump up whatever positive aspect I was able to muster.

The thing that fries me so when I'm in that kind of mood is that it always works. I find something to compliment, or appreciate, or admire about the jerk or situation, and before I know what's hit me I've got a head of steam going. I can actually feel the moment the pivot happens. Valve opened; mission accomplished. Now I can let go, and allow the universe to do its thing.

Porch Light Fury

For a number of years, I rented out a little cottage out back on my property. The deal was that the renters paid for their propane heating, and I paid for electricity.

Well, I had this one young couple who insisted on keeping the front porch light on day and night. I talked to them and talked to them about it. No matter, they'd leave that thing on until I was seeing stars.

It finally hit me that I was dealing with an utterly pointless valve closer. Every time I looked at that cursed light, my valve would slam shut, my dinner would burn, my dogs would start fighting, I'd cut my finger, a loan appointment would cancel, fireplace sparks would singe my rug, and on and on. All while writing this book, no less! Talk about practice what you preach.

So one day—reluctantly—I said, "Okay, I'll find some blasted thing that pleases me about those two and get this valve of mine open." I couldn't. Or more property, I wouldn't. And the light stayed on night after night while I fumed. By now I knew this was serious and had to be spreading like a nasty virus, so with a sulk I decided to look for any blessed thing I could think of that was good about having them there.

"Well...uh...oh, all right, they help me with the yard, and that's a first. They're nice people to have around, so quiet...blah blah, blah." It seemed like searching for a black needle in a wet haystack at midnight, but pretty soon I could feel the resistance softening, and I jumped on it. Bit by grouchy bit I expanded the feeling, and before long I could feel the movement of Feel Better (no, not Feel Good) energy flowing through me. *THEIR LIGHT WENT OUT THAT NIGHT,* and forever after came on only briefly for visitors or groceries! I was flabbergasted. Writing a book about it, sure, yet still amazed and thrilled at the continuing evidence that this stuff really works, even on porch lights.

Was I justified in my annoyed reaction? Of course, but so what?! It was hardly worth screwing up the rest of my world any more than I already had.

Just remember, when you've got negative feelings of *any kind* flowing out (even about porch lights), they're doing a lot more than amplifying that situation. They're acting like the front-line defense of the Dallas Cowboys, blocking all of your Wants from breaking through your massive line of negativity. At the same time, those negative feelings are attracting all sorts of other unpleasant events in the process. Worst of all, if it's a negative person you're getting all riled up about, you're being sucked right into their disconnectedness. How can it possibly be worth it?

Any way you stretch it, no matter what the reason for the negative thought may be, the important thing is that your valve is closed. So get it open!

The Treasure of Touchstones

There will be times when a particular Want/Intent is so foreign to us that we don't know how it would feel, particularly if it's something of an emotional nature or related to spiritual matters such as a closer contact with our concept of God. How do we find the feeling place of something we've so rarely—or perhaps never—experienced?

Or there might be times when all we want is to get out of, or away from, whatever it is we have now, yet we're not sure what it is we want to get *to,* except to feel better than we feel now. How do we find the feeling place of those nebulous kind of things?

There are a couple of ways, and the first one you already know. You fake the feelings of what it might be like to have your desire, talking about it with imagined emotions until your mouth waters, and CLICK! That's the direct way.

The other is indirect, and one I approach with much reverence, for usually the feelings I am calling forth are from deeply cherished and very private memories. We've all had them, those special moments in life we can never forget nor describe, moments we might call an epiphany. They are touchstones, locked away forever in our own secret treasure chest of life's most precious and significant encounters.

On a quiet night, perhaps when the stars are bursting and the air is filled with nightly fragrances, find yourself a comfy spot, relax into the beauty of the moment, and take yourself back in memory to that special time. Or as you sit musing by the window early one morn, watching the sun begin her trek across the skies, go to that touchstone in memory. Go to that never-to-be-forgotten moment in your life and allow yourself to experience its robe of loving remembrance fold about you.

What was the flavor of that touchstone to you? Was it awe, or unspeakable love, or spiritual revelation? Perhaps supreme contentment, or wild joy, or nonsensical frivolity. The feelings need not be labeled, only acknowledged as a treasure of your being.

Then, when you can find no other way to call forth the feelings of your desire, or in moments of despair when you can find no thing to quiet your pain, when you can find no means to feel other than that which you are feeling, go to your touchstone, for there you will find the comfort of unconditional love from your Inner Being/Expanded Self. When your knowledge and your awareness is on that feeling place, you and your Expanded Self are one, and you will no longer be able to focus on your emotional block nor on your pain.

Bring your heart's desire as an offering to this feeling, and immerse that desire reverently into the healing energies of that remembered feeling. Or do nothing except bask in the feelings of that cherished moment. Rest with it, and know that all is well.

The Magic of Appreciation

There are only three states of being we run around in all day long. If we could be even a little more aware of which one we're wearing during each moment of the day, we'd have a big leg up to changing our vibrations.

Victim Mode

This is the oh-dear-they're-doing-it-to-me-again-and-there's-nothing-I-can-do-about-it frame of mind where we go nowhere but around in negative circles, forever magnetizing the same old same old.

Flat-Lining Mode

In the Flat-Lining Mode, we're neither down nor up, just bumping along on second-rate gas. We're not flowing our energy to anything, and surely not attracting anything. In Flat-Lining we're not only living the results of our own erratic flowing of energy, but that of everybody elses. (Like attracts likes, remember?) Very unpleasant! And what most of us do most of the time.

Turned On Mode

Now you're up! You're on! Your high frequencies are no longer attracting the negative vibes of others. You're fueled with the pure positive energy of well-being, vibrating in harmony with your Expanded Self, flowing positive energy out and pulling positive events in while being wrapped in unsurpassed safety and security.

Victim Mode, Flat-Lining, or Turned On, we will always find ourselves in one of the three. Our goal, of course, is to make it the Turned On Mode as often and as long as we can, which is why we look to the high, high energy of *appreciation.*

The vibration of appreciation is the most profoundly important frequency we can hold, for it is the closest thing to cosmic love that exists. When we're appreciating, we're in perfect vibrational harmony with our Source energy, or God energy—call it what you will.

You can jump-start it, or you can jam straight to the feeling, it makes no difference. What's important to know is that *one minute of flowing the intense energy of appreciation overrides thousands of hours spent in Victim or Flat-Lining Modes.*

But take care! No fair just *thinking* appreciation. That won't wash. Thinking is out, feeling is in. You can't just make a decision that you're going to appreciate something and let it go at that. There has to be that surge of significant emotion flowing up from the depths of your being for this to work.

But neither does that mean you have to have just been saved from a life-threatening incident by 911 rescue workers to feel deep appreciation. In fact, flowing appreciation is really no big deal. You can flow it intensely to a street sign if you want. Don't laugh, I do that all the time to stay in shape. Like any skill, flowing energy requires constant practice, and there's something so absurdly satisfying about flowing buckets of love, adoration, and appreciation to "SLOW: MEN AT WORK." I flow it to stoplights, billboards, birds overhead, a tree stump, a dead animal, a winter storm, and of course, to people.

Sometimes in the supermarket I'll pick the meanest looking low-life I can find and just open up and douse the unsuspecting soul with the highest vibration I can muster. Maybe it's appreciation, maybe it's honest-to-God love. One time I did that to a scroungy old biddy who looked like she'd rather eat me than let me pass. I blasted her, and in that very moment she wheeled around, searching angrily for whatever she felt hit her,

151

while I smiled back in pure innocence.

That's my "Hug-A-Bum" game where I envision me and a perfect stranger on the street (or wherever) rushing into each other's arms like we were old best friends who hadn't seen each other for ages. You start with acceptable "targets," like someone you wouldn't mind sitting next to at a lunch counter if you had to. Then you move up, bit by bit, to targets that are increasingly difficult for you socially, until finally it doesn't make any difference what kind of slobs they are.

You just see—and deeply feel—the two of you joyfully recognizing each other and flying together in this gigantic bear hug as profound love surges between you. I don't know how many people I've done that with while walking down a street, and watched them turn around to look for whatever it was they felt.

The vibration of appreciation is also the highest, fastest vibration we can use for attraction. If we would shoot appreciation at anything and everything...all day long...we'd be guaranteed to have heaven on earth in no time, living happily ever after with more friends, more money, more beautiful relationships, in total safety, and closer to the God of our Being than it's possible to fathom.

Be in Love

Ah, "The One" has finally come into your life. You're walking on air with your head in the clouds, consumed with such a euphoric feeling, it defies description. You're in love!

Nothing bothers you. The world is sweet, the day is glorious, it's spring in the middle of winter. Strangers are beautiful. You're floating. You're in love!

Did you know that you can turn that feeling on at will? I don't mean the heightened sexual sensations, but the emotional intoxication, the heady elation. You can walk right out your front door and be in love, and I'm here to tell you that nothing, but nothing feels as good or will raise your vibrations as fast as that.

From there, you can either float on that vibration all day, knowing you are pulling in your Wants, or you can put a specific Want right in the middle of that head-in-the-clouds feeling, flowing your newly spiked energy right out to your oncoming desires.

Remember your first love, how everything seemed to fall into place for you? Problems seemed trivial in a world overflowing with newness, like God just polished the sky.

Be there again. Be in love, and you'll feel yourself come intensely alive. The only thing missing will be the sexual turn on; other than that, everything else will replicate the real thing, because it is the real thing. It's what You are; all you're doing is plugging back in. Besides that, it's a barrel of fun to pretend. And while you're at it, notice the buzz it brings to your body, and that quiet stirring in pit of your tummy.

Always the Sweetness

When all else fails, when you've tried to pull up even a tiny bit of Feel Better with no success, then here's something to remember.

Whether male or female, there is within you a soft-ness, a gentleness, a sweetness so beautiful you might weep from the feeling, were you to touch it. Aggressive or tender, beggar or billionaire, we all have it, for it is what we are. This sweetness has nothing to do with personality. It's not about being weak rather than strong, a doormat rather than a mighty general. It has to do with you, for it is what you are.

To awaken this presence (usually well hidden), you need only put in the request. Make it a Want, or an Intent, then wait, listen, perceive, and allow yourself the experience. Once you have felt this sweetness, this preciousness within yourself, you'll be able to call up the sensation in a moment, anytime you wish. However, it takes extraordinary grit to permit yourself to *live* it, for in this gentle place is the highest vibration of all that you are. Once you have found this naturalness, you have come Home to yourself. Your world will never be the same, for you will never be the same. And neither will your vibrations.

On Downest Days

As long as we live in these bodies, down days are going to happen. On those days when nothing is going right (and you could care less anyhow), just remember that a rotten day is nothing more than a closed valve. You're having a negative energy orgy. It's not a big deal, go on and have it. Give yourself permission to experience the whole bloody downer, so that no negative feelings get stuffed.

But if you really do want out of the vibrational gloomies, then one way to do it is to let your eyes fall on the smallest, most insignificant thing you can find, jump-start with your physical smile, reach down to your Gentle Inner Smile and love that little no-thing in any way you can.

Maybe it's just a speck of dust, or a magazine, or a wire cord. Flood appreciation to it for just being, wrap it in love as if it were the most revered treasure of your life which had been long lost and now is found. You'll be amazed at how easily your vibrations will change.

That fairly unstrenuous approach usually works for me, but if it doesn't, I resort to my never-fail technique where I start dancing around the house, singing some silly up song like "Happy Days Are Here Again" (when I'd rather be screaming at my poor dogs), or "Oh What a Beautiful Morning" (when I'd rather be collapsed on the chair in tears), or some goofy little ditty I make up as I force myself to move around.

I use this ploy when I'm completely down in the pits but no longer willing to stay there. However, when I'm this down, it generally takes a few hours for much of anything to work, so that wild dancing becomes a real starter. It literally cracks open the stuck energy to where I can eventually click back into Feel Much Better. Then, within hours, the phone starts ringing, business picks up, friends invite me over, and ideas start to gurgle again. It's always worked. The point is, do anything you can think of to help you *feeeel* better.

Also, when you're clearly down, tender-talking to yourself reassuringly by name works wonders; "It's going to be okay, Corky, I promise; everything's going to be all right. You're going to be fine." Just talk...about anything that's soothing...until you feel better.

One small gentle step at a time when you're really down; a little here, a little there. It may take a couple of hours or a couple of days, but eventually you'll feel your resistance lessening, and that wonderful click back into open-valve connectedness.

Turn On, Turn On, Turn On!

No matter where you are, you can always turn on with some kind of warm feeling if you really want to.

Turn on as you look out the kitchen window. Turn on as you walk out the door in the morning. Turn on as you slide into your wheelchair. Turn on as you board the subway. Turn on as you sweep the porch. Turn on as you make copies. Turn on as you walk down the fairway. Turn on as you feed the stock.

Until you can find that buzz of joy, or buzz of appreciation, or being in love, or gratitude, even when common sense says you haven't a thing to be grateful for, you're not flowing your energy to anywhere you want to go. But if your desire is to blast out into a new life for yourself, then learn to turn on any way you can, no matter what's happening around you. *NO MATTER WHAT!*

If you want to change something, if you want to improve where you are, if you want that magnificent feeling of fulfillment, or to feel a depth of happiness not normally known to you, if you want to have whatever it is you don't have now, then learn to get your motor running, and turn on!

the force
IS with you

(Step Four)

A few decades ago when I was much newer to life and very new to California, I'd drive day after day from the San Fernando Valley over beautiful Coldwater Canyon into Beverly Hills where I had a funky job in the corporate office of a major aerospace company. I adored the drive, but not the job. However, it wasn't the right time in my life to be rocking boats, since most of my energy was going into working my new Alcoholics Anonymous program, and I was loving every moment of it. For two years I drove the canyon, searched for things to do on my job, and had a blast getting sober in Los Angeles. Then I got bored.

One beautiful afternoon as I was enjoying the drive back to the Valley past the gorgeous homes of Beverly Hills, I said out loud to the power I thought then was only outside of me, "Okay, Higher Power, let's see how well you operate. I'm bored at work and want to do something else. Give me an idea. In fact, if you'll just give me the seeds, I'll plant them."

Without realizing it, I was in that perfect feeling place where my frequency was higher than a kite, loving my drive, enjoying the scenery, feeling at peace with the world yet a little feisty with this being my A.A. friends and I called Higher Power. Sort of like, "All right, Buster, either put up or shut up!" But the statement was sincere and shot out into the ethers powerfully magnetized with high vibrations of impish Feel Good.

The next day on my way to work I went through the same routine. "Just give me the seeds and I'll plant 'em." And again coming home. I didn't know squat about vibrations or flowing energy then, and sadly, I didn't know a thing about my own power, or that the power "out there" and I were one and the same. As far as I was concerned, the Head Honcho was separate from me, that wise force of Good I was quite sure was running my life. All I was doing was powerfully, though unknowingly, focusing on a Want and testing my Higher Power to see if it was really there to lend a helping hand.

Then one wonderous homeward-bound day as I crested the top of the hill where the vista explodes into a thrilling see-forever panorama, the idea hit me, and I do mean hit. I felt as if I had been socked with a cosmic two-by-four. The idea was to form an educational publishing company using the very new and highly innovative audio tape cassette. It was 1965. Most of the world had never heard of a tape cassette, and I didn't have a clue how to form a company or make things start to happen.

No matter. Every day coming home over the hill I'd recite, "Okay, Higher Power, you just keep giving me the seeds, and I'll find ways to plant them." And sure enough, every day without fail, going back over the hill to work, ideas would be going off in my head like roasting popcorn. I was envisioning magazines on tape, auto tape tours of national parks, sales training programs and programs for school kids. For as long as I took that drive, ideas seemed to envelope me, because as long as I took that drive, I was in a Feel Good place, my valve was wide open, and inspiration was easy to access.

The spiral had begun. The more the ideas poured in, the more excited I'd get; the more excited I'd get, the more the ideas poured in. I was buzzing without even knowing it.

People who knew about audio tape cassettes and forming companies started appearing out of nowhere: financial people, legal people, technical people, marketing people, all poking their heads up out of the blue. It was incredible. I finally left the aerospace company to form Listener Corporation, and we became one of the pioneers in dispensing information via the innovative new audio tape cassette.

But pretty soon the excitement wore off, the fear of making it on my own took over, and my flow of inspiration dried up like a desert after a flash flood. The long, slow downward spiral had began, even in the midst of our growing renown.

We were the first company to put auto tours on tape for national parks, and they bombed. We were the first company to put an original monthly business magazine on tape. That took a year before it fizzled. We were the first to have business-related materials on headsets in transcontinental flights, and that bombed. We were one of the first to offer high-powered sales motivational trainers in package form to various industries. That bombed. The formula was simple: fear within me that these things wouldn't work equaled...they didn't!

We finally found our niche with a much less public (and far less fearful) program: in-service training packages for elementary teachers, as well as audio-visual educational materials for elementary education. We became well known, highly respected, loaded with happy sales reps and delighted customers, and I could barely make my mortgage payments.

I'd bang, I'd whack, I'd pound, I'd hammer and I'd push any way that came to mind. I was Hi Ho Silvering all over the place, yet the harder I'd try to attack a problem, the slower would be our progress. Our new programs were receiving electrifying raves coast to coast, and with good reason; they were extraordinarily good, utilizing the finest educational minds of the day and the most innovative approaches to learning. But rave reviews notwithstanding, not one of our programs ever soared into that heady land of really big profits.

All I could think was, "What else can I *DO-DO-DO* to make this thing happen?" The harder I worked, the more fearful I became. And of course the greater my fear, the more resistant I was to the energy of well-being, so the more I was magnetizing my fears of less-than-smashing sales.

Intuitive guidance had gone out the window. There was not the tiniest crack for my Expanded Self to jump in with those fantastic nonstop tips I had once received. I shouted constantly at this so-called Higher Power, telling it where it could get off, and vibrating so far out of alignment with it that I might as well have been nonexistent. I seemed to be right in the middle of that old saw, "The worse it gets, the worse it gets." Brother, was that ever true.

This went on for thirteen years until, exhausted and totally disconnected from anything remotely resembling my Source of well-being, I sold the company and tried to run away to an isolated hideout up the coast by the sea. Instead, I ran smack-dab into the lowest, most painfully disconnected years of my life. From that dark place came the fervent knowing of what I surely did *not* want any longer, and soon there blossomed the years that were to become the most fantastically beautiful of my life as I began to discover my Expanded Self.

The only reason I'm recounting this from-great-to-grim story is because it's a classic demonstration of the hugely different outcomes that occur between *inspired action* and *fear-based action*. With the former, we sail off into happyland with apparently very little effort, as I did when getting the company started. With the latter, we can push and shove and strive and hustle until the cows come home, only to end up going either nowhere...or down.

Inspired Versus Whacking

Most of us have always had this notion—well, it's more than a notion, we were raised that way—that in order to obtain the things we desired to have, we had to match the level of those desires with equivalent personal efforts.

163

In other words, if all we wanted was an ice cream cone, that would take only a minimal personal effort on our part. If, on the other hand, we desired to become the first governor of our state heading a brand new political party, we would gear ourselves up for an entirely different level of personal effort called push and shove. Indeed, we have always believed that in order to even come close to obtaining any of the larger, more significant things we desired beyond ice cream cones, it has meant either knocking our brains out to obtain them or forgetting them altogether.

But knocking our brains out means we're into Hi Ho Silvering with grossly uninspired actions. It means we're operating from a purely physical, pushy stance. It means we're into gotta's, and shoulds. It means, in a nutshell, we're forever trying to push rivers upstream blindfolded, without our own higher Guidance. It means we're operating with very closed valves, causing the kinds of internal stress and negative energy flow that can't possibly produce our desired results.

It would seem, then, that the logical approach to getting where we want to go, or making things happen the way we'd like them to happen, is to operate off of guided inspiration instead of the negative vibrations of social-conscious stress. How do we do that? Where do we start? How do we stop whacking?

Well, first comes the inspiration, the ideas. They come because you've been spending more time in those higher frequencies feeling good (or better), buzzing, and turning on.

Then, after flowing goodly amounts of Feel Good energy to one or more of those great new ideas, you start to act on them, yes, but now from a place of hallowed inspiration rather than negative pushing. And so your actions now become as inspired as your idea, and everything that's coming to you is coming from a place of high frequency.

Then Yeow-eee! Something amazing begins to happen. No matter how complex or involved the ideas seem to be, you find them falling into place and flowing along with the ease and sureness of an uninterrupted mountain stream. And why not? Your ideas were inspired; now, too, are your actions to bring those ideas into reality. All from your higher-frequency energy flow.

Let's say one day you're just bippin' along, feeling great, and you get an idea. It's a fantastic idea, just the kind of thing you know would work if you only knew how to do it...or had enough money...or enough education...or enough support...or enough...?

There are only two ways you can go when you get a bucketful of Guidance downloaded on you:

You can say "Oh, that's just nuts...a good idea maybe, but..." and promptly close your valve.

Or, you can decide to shut up and listen, and trust what you're getting.

If you've been regularly stating some Wants, and your valve has been open more than usual, you can bet you'll soon be receiving Guidance in the form of ideas to help direct you toward those Wants. If you decide to go ahead with one of these ideas and follow the course of activities that will continue flowing into you as hunches or concepts, you'll be going into action, yes, but now we're talking *inspired* action vs. Hi Ho Silvering; *inspired* ways to accomplish your goal, *inspired* activities which will be fun, *inspired* techniques and methods which you'll find yourself performing with the greatest of ease instead of trying to push everything upstream against an unyielding current.

So when inspiration hits, or an idea for how to further your Want just happens to slip in one day, start thinking in Can Do's rather than Yea Buts. Never mind the How To's, they'll come once you relax into that higher frequency. Instruction books always accompany inspiration.

Now the flow begins. What it might take a disconnected person years to do, you whiz through in a few months, guided only into the most productive activities by your thoroughly jubilant Expanded Self.

Greased Slides

Right in the middle of that year of years when the mortgage business and income was pouring in so fast it was laughable, I had an idea. I really didn't need any ideas, as my Wants were streaming in faster than I had time to enjoy. Nonetheless, I had an idea, and it blew me away.

The idea came while I was in the shower one night when, for some reason I don't remember, I was really buzzing. And I have to tell you, my first response—out loud—to what came in was "Give me a bloody break! You gotta be kidding!"

The idea was to do an infomercial (a half-hour TV commercial) for an unusually large and complex self-help product that I had not yet created, had never even thought about, and for which I had not the slightest notion where to begin. The whole concept was mad and totally illogical. I was up to my arm pits in a booming mortgage business, in the middle of the biggest year I had ever had, and was suddenly being down-loaded with droves of ideas about producing a TV program about which I knew nothing. Insane! Not to mention that it would cost fourteen arms and a leg to accomplish, take an inordinate amount of talent to coordinate, and be a full-time job for someone who knew what the hell they were doing, which I most assuredly did not. (Never mind I hadn't even turned out the product.)

But my valve was open even though I didn't understand that, my frequencies were high, and everywhere I looked I saw only positive conditions, so the ideas for having fun kept coming, whether I was asking for them or not.

Just four months—*four months!*—after getting the idea...then manifesting the staggering sums of dollars to pay for the lavish production of product...and the sums required for the first-class production of the TV show...and the dollar or two required to purchase extensive coast-to-coast TV time...and the time to write, narrate, act in, and produce it all, I was filming on location with a sizable professional crew. Just four months, that's all it took!

By March of the following year, I was on the air promoting *Life Course 101,* the monumental audio-visual home-study course I had authored on inner growth. Amazing!

I was performing the work of a dozen people, running one business and creating another while authoring and producing an elaborate new program...by myself...in almost vintage years. To be sure, most of my friends thought I had gone mad.

Ah, but what they didn't know was how effortlessly everything was materializing. There was no Hi Ho Silvering, no frantic pushing or shoving. This time I was connected. Everything flowed as if on a greased slide. Pieces fell magically into place. I'd wonder how to do something, the answers would float in, and I'd easily accomplish whatever needed to be done. No fret, no worry, and not a doubt in the world. Truly, I was having a ball.

Sure it was a lot of work, but it was easy work because the plays were being called straight from the sidelines by my Guidance coach. Any problems that came up were solved as fast as they appeared. Everything—for both companies—kept falling into perfect alignment. I was in the flow of Life. I never questioned a new idea or a new direction, for the How To's were always right behind the idea. And never once did I feel down.

Spontaneity became my middle name. I stopped worrying about time. The high frequency magnetics emanating from me were so powerful, they were mobilizing the next circumstances and events for me to walk into almost before I had finished the last ones. I was dazzled by what was happening, yet all I was doing—without knowing it—was flowing positive Feel Good energy and implementing the inspired ideas that were coming in a steady stream. It doesn't get more exciting than that.

The Signs, The Signs, The Signs

How many times have you said to yourself, "I just got a hit (or a hunch, or a gut-feeling) to go there." And so you did; you went there, and then found out it was a good thing you did. You were following your Guidance. Or you got a crazy idea to try such-and-such. And you did. And it was a success because it was fun. You were following your Guidance.

But you don't have to be starting a new business to have ideas, or hunches, or insights. Whether your Want is to find the fastest way around the traffic downtown or to find a new mate, all you have to do is pay attention to the signs that will come to make it happen...*and learn to trust them!*

A phone call that comes out of the blue from an old friend, a TV show you normally don't watch, a feeling you got to read something, or call someone, or take that other road instead. These are all gentle little shoves from your Expanded Self, your Inner/Outer Guidance helping you stay on course towards your joy, even if it's just a better parking place in the rain. You've blasted Feel Good energy out there, mixed it with Wants, created corridors of energy flowing into massive vortexes, and now as you step into those vortexes, the Guidance comes. Your impulses to act —to do this, go there, call them—are coming from the magnetic activity initiated by your focused energy.

Shortly after embarking on this new path of deliberate creation, I was on my way to Portland in my beloved old '77 Mercury Monarch, a car that had been rebirthed many times since I'd had it because I loved the thing. New engines, new this's, new that's. But because of its age, my mechanics had recommended I start using a synthetic oil to reduce wear and tear. That was fine, except not only were synthetic oils somewhat rare at that time, this was some weirdo brand that had to be special ordered out of town.

I hadn't been out of the house farther than the grocery store for ages, and the two-hour drive to Portland was more than welcomed. I put on some of my soaring music and was just about on the edge of high-frequency bliss an hour later, flowing energy to this and that, when I remembered I hadn't put in the much-needed oil. I usually carried a couple of quarts of the oddball stuff in the car, but had forgotten that, too, and the prospect of finding this kind of oil—that was never to be mixed with any other kind, of course—was between zip and forget it along that farmland stretch of freeway in southern Washington.

I drove a few more miles, wondering what to do, when I got a hit to pull off at the next exit. Since I was pretty much following my hunches without hesitation by then, I shrugged my shoulders and pulled off onto a desolate country road not more than a quarter mile from the freeway.

What I found looked like an old abandoned mining town, or ghost town, replete with cockeyed, broken-down buildings all boarded up and so dilapidated they were tilting. I didn't see signs of life anywhere, but for some reason I stopped the car and got out, strangely aware that I was not questioning my decision to pull off the freeway, or thinking things like "what in the hell am

I doing here," but just going along with the strange lead.

Then I saw it and couldn't believe my eyes. Not fifty feet in front of the car was another broken down building with a hastily hand-painted sign that said "Auto Shop." I don't know how I'd missed it when I stopped, yet there it was, right smack in front of me. Dumbfounded, I walked in and asked if they carried any synthetic oil. Yes, they did, but they were sorry that the only kind they carried was Blurp, just the kind I needed. "Yes m'am, our last two quarts, right over there!"

My head was whirling when I got back to the car. Sure, I was thrilled and excited beyond words. Sure, I was overjoyed to see the Law of Attraction so blatantly in action. But truthfully, I was numb. It was all so bloody obvious, so indisputable. My vibrations had been at an all-time peak. Then came a pressing requirement, but without an ounce of resistance such as, "I'm in trouble, I'll never find it, what'll I do?" With my vibrations at that pitch, I had instantly magnetized the solution, receiving loud and clear directions from my Expanded Self in the form of a super-strong hunch which I decided to follow. But man alive, how melodramatic can you get?

How did it happen? Who knows. Who cares! I got the hit, trusted it, acted on it, and it worked.

The point is to get off auto pilot and pay attention. Listen! Stay alert for that little push, watch for signs, tune in to hunches. If it feels good, it's Guidance.

Most of us don't let ourselves believe something can happen unless we can see ahead of time how all the pieces are going to fit together. So start watching for clues. Watch for the masterful coming together as all the missing parts take form and start dropping into place like magic. Now you've entered the uncanny world of synchronicity, you're plugged in, connected to your Source energy, going with the flow. But you'll never see it, or learn to trust it, if you're not watching for it.

Without Hesitation

With the possible exception of prayer, which is more often a plea from a closed rather than opened valve, precious few of us were ever taught to go inside, shut up and listen, much less follow! Follow what? Listen to whom? Nonsense! Take a pill. That's just imagination. It has no substance, no intellectual empirical data to back it up.

I love how we pretend that something doesn't exist, then turn right around and name it. We turn our noses up at "divine guidance," but curiously give it this wide range of names like gut-feeling, motivation, hit, intuition, sense, inspiration, impulse, urge, premonition, desire, imagination. It's all Guidance, the real You sending messages from the infinite intelligence You are, doing everything in Its power to pass on some ideas or direction before you shut down again.

Guidance is Soul-talk, God-talk, Inner Being-talk, Expanded Self-talk, Cosmic Escort-talk. Guidance does whatever is necessary to get our attention and help us step into our Wants, be it oil for the car or new hair for a shining head. But to make it work, we've got to learn to trust what we're picking up on that station.

A couple who were mortgage clients of mine—I'll call them George and Sally—were a little shaken when I got to their home one evening to take their loan application. When I asked what was wrong, George said he and his wife had just missed being in a serious eight-car pile up on the freeway, and they were still feeling "really spooked," as he put it.

They worked at different places, but commuted together. Seems they were coming home from work on the freeway as usual, and George was beginning to get antsy being stuck behind a large, red, wobbly truck in front of them, so he decided to change lanes. Out of nowhere Sally said, "Honey, don't do that! We've got to get off this freeway right now!" There was the customary explosion about how silly that was, then finally, to keep the peace, George turned off at the next exit and headed for some very out-of-the-way back roads.

When they got home, George switched on the local TV news as usual, and saw his wobbly red truck in the middle of a pile up, squashed between two cars not a mile down the freeway from where they had exited. There were two fatalities.

That was one tuned-in lady who followed her Guidance without hesitation. How many of us would have listened, much less acted by taking another road?

The cosmic joke is that we were designed to do just that, to live by our senses, not by our brains. But over the eons we've learned to *think* our responses instead of *feel* them, totally backwards from the way all the rest of nature lives. Animals and plants do it (live by their senses), while all us closed-down, disconnected humans snicker at it. But when you really start playing the Feel Good game, I promise, it's better than an all-day ticket to Disneyland. You listen and do, listen and do, listen and do, trusting your Guidance without hesitation.

So if you have five dozen friends and family telling you to do "this," but your deepest impulse is to do "that," always, always follow your impulse (provided it feels good!). Why? Just do it a few times and you'll see why. Your Guidance system is doing all it knows how to get you where you want to go to follow your Original Intent. So give it a chance. Tune in and listen up; that Expanded Self knows what it's doing.

The Final Step

Therein lies the fourth and final step in this process of creating by design.

The first, you remember, is to identify what we DON'T want.

The second is to clarify and state what we DO want.

The third is to get into the feeling place of those Wants. And now the fourth:

Step Four: Expect it, listen, and
allow the universe to bring it.

Translated that means no more pounding something into place to make it happen. It means we tune in and listen to our Guidance. It means we follow what we get without hesitation.

It means we stop trying to figure out how we could ever make our Want transpire, because we aren't the ones who have to figure it out anyhow. All we have to do is act on the inspirations coming from our Expanded

Self, keep our valve open, expect that our Want is on its way, then step back and let the universe do its thing, staying out of the trap of impatience as much as possible. (For that matter, even staying out of patience, because patience is just a closed valve pretending to be open with all its focus on what hasn't happened.)

The universe is a better organizer than you could ever think of being, so give it a chance and stay out of the way. You've given the universe a task, you've sent out your magnetic energy, now settle back and allow the manifestation to unfold.

But Where the Hell Is It?

Okay, you're keeping your frequencies up, staying tuned to the Guidance station, listening, getting your hunches, watching the synchronicity of events, but where in the Sam Hill *is* this terrific Want of yours?

"How can I stay all revved up and excited about something when I keep talking, feeling, and flowing energy until I'm blue in the face, but nothing happens?"

If your Want hasn't shown up in whatever you consider to be a reasonable amount of time, it simply means you've been more in the feeling place of *not* having it, and less in the feeling place of having it.

That's all right. You're not doing it wrong; you didn't lose the instruction book. The deliberate flowing of positive energy is so foreign to us, it often seems to be an impossible task, while the resistant feelings we're so accustomed to—and therefore never notice—continue to dominate our day.

That's when it's time to let it be okay—*let it be okay*—that your Want hasn't shown yet. You know that it will, but it's perfectly normal that it hasn't...yet.

The ultimate goal, of course, is to stop seesawing with open valves, shut valves, open valves, shut valves. That's like calling a dog and telling him to stay at the same time. Everything jams to a halt. How, then, does one retain passion for something that hasn't shown up or happened?

First, check out what you're flowing energy *to*. There's not much point in flowing energy to—and manifesting more of—any of your Don't Wants.

Next, check out your intensity of energy flow. The greater your excitement, the more ardent your passion; and the more ardent your passion, the faster your manifestation. (Ask your Guidance for help with your passion and you'll get it.)

Next, check your repetitions. How often do you get yourself jazzed about your Want? If you had a great start, got all worked up about it for several minutes and then never thought about it again, it may come someday (though doubtful). But if you keep yourself hyped up about it, talk about it several times a day to yourself, your parakeet and your roses, and embellish the story every time you do, you're not only keeping the momentum going, you're building it.

Although sixteen seconds is all that's necessary to add to the forming vortex, if you'd get turned on and really buzzing about this thing for just ten or fifteen minutes every day, it will be in your face before you know it, *providing* you keep your focus off its absence.

There's something else that goes on in regard to a show or no-show which I hesitate to mention because it can be such a cop-out, such a perfect excuse for why something has not happened or shown up yet, and that is timing. You may have been flowing energy passionately toward a subject with a wide-open valve, doing everything by the book, flowing with the force of a space shuttle rocket and still have a no-show on your hands. Timing! It simply may not be the best time for this Want to happen if you're to derive from it all you desire.

Since that may be the case, then just step back, relax, and let the universe and your Guidance do their things.

The Law of Attraction is never inconsistent. The universe will bring you whatever you want in the appropriate time. The key—always—is focus!

What's Been Bothering Me?

We already know the only thing that messes up our experience is resistance to our own higher energies, but sometimes being in those energies can cause things to happen that are not always too pleasant. Pulling in higher frequency is sort of like aiming a hose at a muddy old sidewalk. The heavy stream of water squirts away the mud to reveal some nasty cracks in the walkway. If you're not careful as you step on the sidewalk now, you might trip over one of those long-hidden cracks.

Those cracks are our resistance, our inner critic or naysayer, our old ideas of social rights and wrongs, our old low-frequency security blankets being laid bare by the higher frequencies. The greater our wanting is, the greater the energy we're pulling in, just as the more forceful the stream of water is, the more cracks will be uncovered. All of a sudden we feel rocky, vulnerable, exposed to the elements without protection as what has been hidden away for so long surfaces to struggle for survival. Ultimately what has been hidden will die away, but not without a fight. This can make for some rather bumpy, emotional rides.

Not to worry, there's a fast way out. The moment you become aware that you're feeling a little shaky or off base, ask yourself: *What's been bothering me?* and keep at it until an answer comes. It will.

As you discuss it with yourself, whatever it is that has been uncovered to cause those unpleasant old feelings to reemerge will show itself in the form of an old belief, an old fear, an old Don't Want. Once you unveil whatever it is, if you'll take just three minutes a day to talk it out and talk it down (as in Tender Talking), talk it out and talk it down, talk it out and talk it down, most of that fear will dissipate within thirty days, along with the unconscious resistance that's been blocking your Want.

Passion Is Creation

Passion. We've talked a lot about it. It's one of those words that sounds great, but what does it mean? How do we get it? And do we really need it?

Here's your clue: passion is creation!

Contentment is swell, but passion makes it happen.

Contentment is an open valve, a nice safe haven with no negative focus, a place of rest. But passion makes it happen. Passion is living. Passion is creation.

Passion is about feeling your power. When negative conditions pop up for whatever reason (as they always will because we require the contrast), instead of talking about how tough things are, dig down and feel your power. You're not only connected to the force of well-being, you *are* that force. That force is Life. That force is passion. And passion is creation.

Passion comes from the excitement of having something in the making. Contentment, on the other hand, comes from looking at something already achieved, more like a satisfaction. Contentment is positive energy, true, but it's not a fuel; it won't take you any place. It is not an energy of creation.

If you think you're lacking this most intoxicating of feelings, passion, check to see if you're still talking about or focused on a Don't Want. There's not a Don't Want in the universe that can evoke passion, for all that Don't Wants will ever get you is negative energy, closed valves, greater resistance, and more Don't Wants.

So here's yet another reason for giving more time to your Want, for the more time you spend on it, the more passionate you will become. And passion is creation.

Passion doesn't mean rah-rah cheerleading, or spastically bouncing off walls. Sure, passion comes in various degrees of excitement and enthusiasm, but more important, passion is a strong inner knowing. It's a quiet sureness that life no longer has you by the ear lobes, and that the tiger you're holding by the tail is actually you!

You want more passion? Then follow your joy! Go smell more roses, watch more sunsets, find more grass to walk barefoot on, visit more favorite restaurants, laugh more, find more places to explore, go to more ball games or plays, indulge in more hobbies, be more spontaneous, play more golf, listen to more music, find more places to skinny dip, smile more, have more fun. Now you're vibrating in open-valve passion. And passion is creation.

Let It Come

Hey, you won't get an argument from me. All this energy business is a total about-face from the way we've been used to living and being, so give it time. Cut yourself some slack. If you've read this far, major changes are already in progress.

Sometimes it will be easy. Most of the time early on it won't be, which is why watching for those so-called coincidences is so important. They are validation that something's actually happening; they keep you going.

Mainly, just lighten up. Be natural. Get off your case for not being perfect. Pat yourself on the back for effort. Give yourself credit for wanting to take control of your life. You will, sooner than you think!

If you're spending some time each day talking about each of your Wants, not worrying about if or when they're coming, not trying to force the how-to's of bringing them in, staying plugged into your Guidance and following it without hesitation, those Wants will come. By your own power, they must.

You are not separate from the power of infinite well-being. You are not separate from the power of creative

Life force. You are not separate from the universal power of All That Is. That power is your power, because that power is You. And your power, like the divine laws by which it is governed, is absolute.

money!
money!
money!

All right, let's get down to it...*MONEY!!!* Money, money, money. Sounds good, doesn't it? Or does it? No, I'm not retarded. Let's put it another way: How does the word—or topic—make you feel? Honestly!

Every word we utter carries its own brand of vibration peculiar to the one doing the speaking. Depending on how we were raised and what our own distinctive outlook on life may be, we charge the words we speak with a personally exclusive vibration. The word "God," for instance, can evoke either a highly positive or powerfully negative vibrational response, depending on who's doing the speaking—or listening—and what their background and association has been with that word.

We have a truckload of these juiced-up words in our language, but there's only one which can lay claim to consistently winning the "Top Negative Word Vibration" award. That word is "money," the most highly charged word in any language that uses the stuff.

With most of us, the beliefs associated with this word are so incredibly intense, the moment we speak, think, or hear it, we send out walloping negative vibrations all over the place. Of course, all that does is create an impenetrable wall around us that guarantees blockage of this most sought-after commodity into our lives. Just by speaking that dumb little grouping of sounds, we're stalling the very thing we most desire.

But how come? This is, after all, pretty neat stuff, is it not? Gold, silver, coins, paper notes, all that jazz?

More like "all that misery." From the time we were tiny tots, at least for the majority of us, we learned that the word money equates to struggle, shoulds, musts, have-to's, gotta's.

We learned how the subject felt to Mom and Dad, to uncles and aunts, to grown-up family friends.

We learned the anxiety that surrounds the word, and the anguish.

We learned, for the most part, that it is the be-all and end-all of what we believe to be life, so we had better make damn sure we have it, or else!

Actually, that learning curve began well before toddler days, back in the womb where we absorbed all the many vibrations of our parents' struggles and fears. So we came bouncing into the world like Don Quixote with this cockeyed inborn programming that says the greatest adversary we shall ever confront in life will be this thing we call money, the dragon against which we must war unto death. And most of us do!

Because we never learned about flowing energy and getting out of negative vibrations, we spend our lives with thoroughly closed valves over this subject, fighting a battle we can't possibly win until we become so tired, so discouraged, so downtrodden, our body finally responds to the perpetual negativity, and we die. Swell life!

Screw Old Beliefs

Ever since legal tender was first created, no one has had enough. So as we think money, we immediately think "not enough," and now can you start to see the picture? Money equates to not enough...which equates to lack...which equates to Feel Bad vibrations...which faithfully supplies us more of precisely what we don't want any more of: lack!

The good news is we don't have to get in there and dig up all our moldy old beliefs about money to allow the abundance to flow; we only have to override them. And thank heavens for that; we'd be on the couch for decades trying to overcome the plethora of well-ensconced doctrines about money that society has so unjustly created, like:

"You have to work hard to get it."

"Money must be earned."

"You don't get something for nothing."

"Money is hard to come by."

"Money is hard to save."

"I never have enough."

"It goes out faster than it comes in."

"Money is the root of all evil."

"We need to save for retirement."

"I'll be happy when I get it" (meaning "I can't be happy now").

"One must strive hard for the real rewards."

"Money doesn't grow on trees."

Repeat any one of those phrases out loud and see how you feel. Not good! Yet that's the stuff we were raised on, all so vibrationally ingrained in us that we think money is our only key to freedom. And hey, I'm not arguing that. What trips us up is we think it has to be earned, fought for, worked hard for, struggled for. Yet money, like anything else, is nothing but energy. And attracting it, like anything else, is nothing more than an energy-flowing process.

Now is when you write a new script.

Writing a New Script

Let's say you used to think about having an extra $25,000 for a bunch of things you wanted to do. And let's say you would think about the money, and think about it, have no idea how to get it, feel frustrated and perhaps even a little inadequate, and finally forget it.

You were acting just like all the rest of us, bumping up against so many uncomfortable old beliefs that have been lifelong valve closers for you, you finally said, "To hell with it," and shut down. Your desire for the money felt bad, so you stopped thinking about it, and of course never got it.

Needless to say, that was before you knew about flowing energy. So let's say you think about that $25,000 now. Sure, you probably still get some of the same negative feelings, only this time you can spot them because you've been paying attention to how your thoughts make you feel. This time, instead of staying in those downer feelings, you write a new script, pasting a whole new vibrational page over the old one.

Writing a new script is nothing more than making up a grand little story to tell yourself and stepping into it emotionally. That's the important part: you have to get into into your story *emotionally,* or you're just blowing hot air.

This new script of yours is an intriguing, fun little story about what you're going to do with the dollars when you have them, a story so real to you, you can feel the excitement and practically taste the results. Just by your telling of this little story, you begin to visualize, then feel; visualize and feel, visualize and feel. That's the whole point, to *feeeel* what you're concocting. No feel...no get! Because, no feel...no vibrational change.

Your story can be utterly make believe or absolutely true, it doesn't matter, since it's the joyful emotions behind your words that cause the positive vibrations necessary to make this all happen. So make believe or not, you're creating a new magnetic focal point—or vortex—with your fresh images and warm feelings. Just don't make your story so unbelievable that you can't get into the feelings, or you've defeated your whole purpose.

As the vortex begins to grow from the first sixteen seconds of happy storytelling, and the next sixteen seconds, and the next, the high vibrations flowing out from you begin to cancel out the lower vibrations of the ones you're living in now, completely overriding your current "what is." When that switch-over to a higher frequency kicks in, the entire universe begins to respond to your heightened vibrations. At this point, everything you need to bring your made-up little story into reality—including you—is being drawn into that new vortex created from the pure delight of your storytelling.

Now granted, you may feel a little silly at first telling yourself this quaint little bedtime story out loud (always out loud!), but that's a small price to pay for increased income. Just start talking, making up this fun tale about all the many different things you're going to do with that $25,000 when you get it. Take it slow, allowing yourself plenty of time to *feeeel* the words and pictures as you move along, and plenty of time to allow more and more ideas for uses of the money to pop in. Remember, this is just make believe, so you have no reason to doubt anything that comes up.

It's sometimes easier to call yourself by name when you're scriptwriting, rather than saying "I." The word "I" is another one of those painfully charged words holding a vibrational bag of unworthiness junk, so you may find more freedom in calling yourself by name. Either way will work; just use whichever is most comfortable.

Your story might go something like this:

"There's a bright, good-looking fellow by the name of Jack who lives with his wife in a wonderful town filled with friendly people, and in a beautiful home filled with many loving treasures. (Long and slow; *feeeeel*ing it all the way along.)

"Jack has a good job that he enjoys (remember, this is make believe), and he's always made an adequate living. He's a bright man, loving, kind, and, oh yes, very, very good looking.

"Well, one day Jack and his wife decided it was time to treat themselves to some things they had wanted for a long, long time, so they agreed to take the extra money they had in the bank, and spend it on some fun, well-deserved projects.

"They had always wanted to build a patio on the back of their house, so that was their first project. They had so much fun designing and planning it that they just knew it would turn out to be what they had always wanted. (Describe the patio in minute detail). And indeed it did.

"Now that the patio's finished, Jack and his wife love to sit out under the stars at night and talk. They seem to be closer than ever, and they both believe it's due to their patio. The smells in the air are so sweet in the cool of the evening..."

...and on...and on...and on, slowly feeling each new awareness of the same topic, savoring each delicious moment of description.

You've got to give that money outlets to flow to, so tomorrow when you do this, talk about the next project, and the next day about the vacation trip, and then about the new car, and about the final payment on the new boat, savoring and appreciating each little thing as you talk and feel, talk and feel, talk and feel.

You've taken the $25,000 out of the old Feel Bad scripting and created a shiny new dream script to paste over it, one that is genuinely overflowing with all sorts of easy to believe, Feel Good energy, though still only a story.

Caution: If you find yourself closing down while scripting, you've just stumbled up against one of your old pieces of baggage. No problem. Just ask yourself "What's bothering me?" and talk it out gently until the script feels good again. Also, be alert for statements that are actually Don't Wants, such as "...and Jack didn't want to have to work so hard." If one like that pops out, simply turn it around to a Want. And by the way, you can play this game with a loving partner *provided* you're both on the same wavelength, wanting the same types of things. Two of you doing this will actually magnify the energies tenfold, and spark all manner of new ideas to get your juices running.

Of course scripting is not just about money; you can script for anything: a trip to Fiji Island, a new relationship, or getting rid of moles in your yard.

My dog, Lucy, was driving me bonkers, running up and down the long front fence, barking at anything that moved. It was tiresome to me, annoying to the walkers, and infuriating to my neighbors. I tried every maneuver in the dog books, but nothing seemed to work. Finally, worn down and really a bit concerned (which only caused more barking), I ventured into writing a new script.

"Lynn loves to watch the free spirit in her dog run wild as the wind, up and down the front fences. And most of all, Lynn loves to watch her dog come to a rest, and sit at the fence line quietly watching the walkers go by, so attentive, so well-behaved. After all, Lucy is in charge of Lynn's property, and it is her unassigned job to guard this property, which she does to perfection by sitting hushed and alert and watching."

I went through that routine every day, seeing myself praise Lucy for racing up on our side of the fence to

190

whatever was moving on the street, coming to a screeching halt, and then just sitting in silent watch.

Five weeks dragged by before I saw the first sign. Lucy didn't even run! She just sat in the driveway and watched this guy jog past. She just sat there! All in all, the whole process took about three months, which goes to show how strong my old beliefs were about not being able to change such a stubborn dog, etc., etc. But I stuck with it, and as of this moment at least, we are two very happy beings.

When it came to money, though, my first attempts at scriptwriting weren't anywhere near that successful. I was trying so hard to paint surrealistic pictures of dollars pouring in that I was burying myself under a mountain of totally unbelievable stories. I could feel my old belief systems raising their doubting heads with stuff like "How on earth are you going to do that? Where will you get the time? What if no one is interested?" Doubt, doubt, doubt.

Gradually, it sank in that I didn't need to create a multimillion dollar Steven Spielberg production number, just a moderately believable little story. So I started over again with a greatly toned-down tale that was much more credible to me. Instead of talking about money pouring in, I gave it outlets to flow to. I talked about how easy it was beginning to be paying my bills, how nicely all my projects were falling into place, how my mortgage programs were being so well received in the market. That felt good.

I told me a new twist on the same story every day for weeks, creating new characters to keep the thing alive, or sometimes creating a whole new story line

191

that seemed to trip in from left field. I'd let myself get discouraged, wonder what I'd been suckered into, realize I was right back into negative, give out a big sigh, and start scripting again.

Then it broke open. I got some astounding—in fact, revolutionary—new ideas to bring in four times the business with half the usual effort. New people popped in to help out, and in about six months I was back on track again making a comfortable living; not mammoth, but comfortable. Yes, it took a while to get back where I wanted to be; old habits die hard, but die they did.

So if you have a hankering to travel, never mind how you're going to get the dollars, just start writing your script and flowing Feel Good energy to where you want to go. Feel the breezes, taste the food, wear the tan.

If you always wanted to own a race horse, never mind how you're going to get the dollars. Start writing your script and flowing Feel Good energy to the kind of horse you want, and the trainer, and the facilities. Feel the mane, smell the horse smells, wear the roses.

If you and your spouse have always wanted to live a more simple life running a bed and breakfast in the country, then pick out the perfect place, walk the gentle country roads, marvel at the fresh air, chat with the contractors who are helping you remodel the home, choose the darling wallpaper, find the antiques, enjoy your happy guests, and cook up a splendiferous brunch for everyone.

That's really all there is to it. You replace the old negative vibrational script that's running you now which vibrates "I can't, it's silly, I'm crazy," with a positive new one. You write or speak it *and feel it* the way you want it to be, staying with the new story until you've felt it click in. Now you are no longer a reactor *to* conditions, you have become a creator *of* conditions.

From No Biz to Big Biz

A good friend of mine owns a sizable independent real estate firm in Washington state. He's always been a hard worker, fair to his employees and supportive to his agents, but he was having some financial problems and couldn't seem to find a way out.

Over lunch one day, Chuck started talking. The whole area was in a prolonged slump, and everybody's sales were down. Even his best agents were talking about leaving to go into other fields of business. Everyone knew the market would turn around eventually, but in the meantime there were mouths to feed.

My friend wasn't looking for answers, because it seemed to him that there were none. To his way of thinking, he had become a victim of economic circumstance. He and his crew had exhausted all the usual promotional gimicks and pounded all the proverbial pavements only to watch sales continue their avalanche downward. Although I had never talked with Chuck about the Law of Attraction, I figured this was as good a time as any, since I knew him well enough to know he'd at least be polite and listen.

It seemed the biggest problem was not so much that sales weren't happening, but that his sales people weren't happening either. They were down in the sewer someplace with very closed valves feeling grossly sorry for themselves, blaming the economy, creating an enormous group vortex of lack, and absolutely guaranteeing the company's continued slide into oblivion. So I suggested that Chuck have one more meeting with his people to point out that since they had tried everything else, there was little for them to lose in trying this one last project on for size.

Only touching lightly on the physics of the Law of Attraction, I looked him right in the eye and spoke from my soul, hoping my uncharacteristic seriousness might get his attention. "Chuck, if you can get your people to do this, your business will turn around."

It worked! I had to admit feeling a bit smug as I watched him so earnestly reply, "Go on."

I suggested he have each of his people pick a dollar number of what they'd like to make in the next three months, and then triple it. (Chuck groaned an "Oh God, here we go again," but I ignored it.) Then I suggested that once they all had that figure in mind, Chuck should ask each one *why* they wanted the money, staying with one person at a time and working it through with him, because once that first guy got the routine, the rest would know how to dive right in. (His pained look mellowed into "hummm, interesting!")

Without going into detail, I explained that their first responses would probably be Don't Want's coming from a place of lack, and that statements like "I want the money so I can pay my bills" would only get them more of the same—no money and more bills.

Chuck wasn't getting it, so I got him talking while I asked the Whys. "All right, my friend, tell me what you

194

want right now."

"I want to pay my bills."

"Why?"

"So I can feel better."

"Why?"

"Because I hate being uptight."

"Why?"

"Because it makes me feel bad?" (Getting close.)

"So how would you rather feel?"

"Free! I want to feel free!" EUREKA! We had it!

"Okay, make it a statement."

"I want to have $60,000 so I can feel free."

"Great! Now how does that feel?"

"Oh, it feels fine for a minute, but good grief! How would I ever get that kind of money in this market?"

"Forget the money. It's only a grubby pile of paper. Talk to me about what you'll do with the money after the bills are paid."

Bit by bit, a long-hidden collection of dreams unfurled. He and his wife, Sara, would go to Bermuda where they had always wanted to explore the possibility of retirement. They'd take the grandkids on a cruise somewhere. They'd turn the basement into a full-blown stereophonic music room. And on and on.

But the one I could tell he really perked on was Bermuda, so I wanted him to dive into that one. I put on my most earnest face and leaned across table as far as I could stretch. "Tell me in detail, Chuck. Every little detail you can think of about the dreams you and Sara have of retirement in Bermuda."

It was awesome. The whole room lit up as Chuck's energy soared to the heavens. It was as if he had never dared open his heart to this subject, so the more the words and feelings poured out, the wider his valve opened. Chuck wasn't flowing energy to his Want, he was blitzing it.

Right in the middle of his reverie, I said, "Hold it! That feeling place where you are right now is where I want you to bring each of your sales people. Tell them to forget the actual paper dollars they've specified and start focusing instead on what things the dollars could bring them. Then start flowing energy towards those things until they reach the same passion you just experienced. This way you've got them sneaking in the Feel Good back door. By avoiding any of the negative connotations usually associated with dollars—especially when they're out of them—they'll unconsciously allow the cash to magnetize in.

"Your people want what we all want, Chuck: not the stupid pieces of paper, but the experiences that come with having them. Make them promise they'll do this for thirty days, at least once every day for ten or fifteen minutes."

To my total delight, Chuck called about six weeks later with the first good news. His people had been so down, he had had no trouble in cajoling them into his little experiment.

But that wasn't too surprising, since I had coached Chuck into doing some "prepaving." I told him how to create that initial meeting in his mind just the way he wanted it to happen—including that his people be open and willing—and to flow that kind of "up" energy to it. He did, and by the time everyone gathered together, they were nowhere as resistant as they might have been had Chuck not helped them along vibrationally.

Everybody except one upheld their promise and was faithfully flowing Feel Good energy every day to their Wants as they wrote new scripts. They had genuinely gotten into the swing of this thing, and started feeling a lot more enthusiastic about life without a clue as to why. They felt better, so who cared what the reason was.

About ten weeks into the venture, sales started to develop, but from off-the-wall sources. One gal had an aunt in Illinois who wanted to move to Washington. Another had an Army son and his friends who had just been transferred to the local base at Fort Lewis and wanted Mom to find houses for all of them. Another fellow had two referrals come in from a person he thought would never speak to him again. And still another had big success with a marketing idea to contact a very select group of buyers.

Everybody had some kind of movement going, enough for them to see there was no way all these happenings could be called coincidence. In the face of one of the worst real estate markets in the area's history, these folks had found they could circumvent conditions and be responsible for their own destiny.

Every day this gang was connecting to their Inner Beings/Expanded Selves, feeling inspired for the first time in months. They were sending out highly charged waves of positive energy to the universe with their individual Requisition Lists, and the universe was responding with circumstances, incidents, ideas, and motivation in accordance with their levels of intensity.

Best of all, it became infectious, and apparently still is.

(The guy who didn't care to participate in the experiment ended up quitting the business. The last we heard, he was living off his wife's retirement income.)

The $100 Trick

An old belief—or any belief—is a nothing but a vibrational habit that we respond to like trained seals.

Put another way, we have pretty strong attachments (beliefs) to what we've been taught, and even stronger attachments to what we've lived. Yet those old beliefs we hang on to, and respond to, are nothing more than the way we used to think life worked, like having to struggle.

For instance, something comes up in our world, hits an old belief, and we start vibrating negatively over this thing out of sheer habit. *Just out of habit!*

So our goal here is to find anything at all to break those old vibrational habit patterns of thought. Well here's a pip. It falls under that same category of needing to provide ample outlets for money to flow to, meaning, we've got to give the energy of money oodles of outlets to flow through and to before it can start flowing all around us. Judging from my own, as well as my friends' experiences, this one's a sure winner.

Get a hundred dollar bill—or the biggest bill you can possibly afford (don't skimp!)—and stick it in your wallet. Now, go shopping.

If you can manage a full day, great. If not, go for a lunchtime in the mall, or someplace where there are lots of shops. You're looking for everything you'd like to buy with that $100. Maybe it's a Walkman, or a pair of slacks, or a football, or a new dress, or some tools, or a bed cover; anything at all that turns you on that you'd like to own.

You still have that $100 in your pocket, so you say to yourself *(while you feeeeel your delight),* "Wow, I could buy that with my $100; no problem!"

"Oooo, terrific, I could buy that!"

"Man, that's just what I've always wanted, and I have the money to buy it!"

You're not adding up the items to come to $100; you're looking for all the individual $100 items you could actually buy right now with that $100 if you wanted to.

By the time you're up to somewhere around a thousand items, look what's happened. You've just emotionally spent $100,000 which is going to go a long way toward helping you *feeeeel* prosperous, overriding a flock of those old vibrational thought patterns about lack.

My friend Jocelyn was dangerously close to some serious financial problems, going through one of those frustrating periods of "it's not happening fast enough." Although she knew full well that that sort of attitude was contributing to "it" staying away, she couldn't seem to break the vibrational habit pattern. Then one day she remembered the $100 trick. Almost the instant she thought about it she hopped in her car, left her cows and chickens to their own meanderings, and headed straight out of town for the biggest mall in the state, quite a distance from her home.

Joce spent almost the whole day getting more and more jazzed with this silly little game, forcing herself to let go, relax, have fun with it, and emotionally "spend, spend, spend."

Finally, exhausted but filled with the vibrations of a very open valve from the thrill of the hunt, she came home to find (I swear...this is a true story!!) a message from her brother offering to help out financially; a message from a friend offering to help out financially; and a message that the loan on her house—which had been turned down twice because of the very unusual home in which she lived—was now approved and ready to fund within a few days. Plus, she had gotten the idea for a whole new sales approach to her business on the way home. Not bad for a few hours of play.

Prepaving – The Quick Shot

If you truly desire a less bumpy walk in your daily life, you gotta give that energy of yours more outlets, more things to flow to in order to keep it moving. One terrific way to do that is by "prepaving."

Prepaving isn't for cruises and castles and custom cars. Prepaving is used more for intangibles, for creating a desired environment or atmosphere in order that a particular event or happening can come about. It's more "this is the way I want it to happen" energy you flow to a stream of daily happenings and decisions like:

"I intend to roll into a close-in parking place at the show tonight."

"I intend to get my report finished with ease, and on time."

"I intend to enjoy the day."

"I intend for my lunch meeting to be successful for both sides. And enjoyable!"

"I intend that the animosity between us be resolved, and soon."

This is prepaving, sending out your vibrational intents ahead of you—with feeling—to arrange your day and circumstances as you desire them to be.

Prepaving is much like writing a new script, only not so involved. It's a quick shot. When you've gotten used to prepaving with little things on a daily basis, start in with the larger business snags—maybe a client you're having trouble with or a sale that's been on hold. Spend some time seeing and *feeeeeling* the way you want the meeting to go or the contract to be signed: seeing and *feeeeeling*, seeing and *feeeeeling* in a series of quick shots throughout the day.

A friend of mine did some prepaving with a court case he was facing where he knew he was sure to lose. Instead of seeing himself winning, which he couldn't imagine (with good reason), he saw and felt everybody coming up winners, shaking hands, patting each other on the back, etc. Sure enough, the case was settled to everybody's satisfaction a few days before going to court.

Another friend—a young one—had a boss who was bugging her about her attire. Apparently, boss didn't like short skirts, and my friend had the misfortune of being the first to show up in one. Really put off by his attitude, she finally did some prepaving, with a totally humorous outcome. Instead of boss ignoring her attire completely, as my young friend was visioning and feeling, he switched gears into open flattery as three other girls donned similar outfits. Hey, whatever it takes.

Got a desk piled high with work? On overload with details? Prepave the day to go with ease before you get there. See yourself breezing through the work. Speak your Intent and tell the universe why you want it. Then don't you dare pick up one piece of paper until you flow buckets of positive energy to get that valve of yours open, or you'll be right back in the overload soup.

Prepaving is simply sending your energy ahead of you, programmed with the frequency of your desire. Sometimes you send it to a specific place, sometimes you spray it around, other times you send it to a person. Granted, you can't change somebody's mind, force them to act against their will, or do anything that's against their nature. But in tense situations, you can prepave to create an atmosphere of trust and openness which will spawn congeniality. The groundwork is done; the rest is up to you—and your Guidance—when you get there.

Tell the universe what you want, flow a batch of pure positive buzzing to it, *feeeeel* what it would be like to have it come about, then know it's going to happen. That's prepaving.

The Universe as Sales Manager

Business is slow, and you want to generate more profits. Maybe you're thinking you should add more sales staff, or merge, or go for a bigger ad budget; all the same old alternatives to the same old question, how to generate more black ink.

Here's a suggestion. Get some group energy going to square itself. Unlike Chuck's crowd, which focused on individual outcomes, your people script their desire for the *company* (which will ultimately be for themselves).

What you're going for is group magnetics. The focused energy of any group squares itself in strength, whether positive or negative energy, so you could be talking some incredible dynamics here. If you have only two people with their energy focused on one goal, that energy squares itself by two, so it becomes the equivalent of four. However, if you have a bunch of people blasting away at one goal, now you're talking serious magnetics, and a tremendous potential for change, providing most don't revert back to "can't be done" kind of thinking.

Contrary to the widespread belief held since the industrial revolution, generating more dollars above the line is not about hiring more sales staff to whack out the sales; it's about getting the staff you have into the habit of expectation by mentally and emotionally writing new corporate scripts. Every successful company has done precisely that, no matter what they've called it in house: brilliant contract, terrific ad campaign, good pricing, dazzling product, motivated sales staff. If the majority of employees don't expect it to happen, it won't.

However, if you can get everyone in your group feeling the excitement of a contract being awarded, feeling pride for the guy who got it signed, seeing/feeling a considerable new crowd of customers in the store, seeing success happening while feeling the value of their own contributions to that success, the exponential force of this type of magnetics is colossal. It will change forever the way you do business.

Just Remember...

- It's not about money; it's about how you're flowing your energy. The money will come when you stop looking at how much of it you don't have. You can't look at "not enough money" and feel anything but negative emotion, which disallows the flow. So find more ways to open your valve.

- Instruction books always accompany inspiration, so forget the "How To's." They'll appear.

- Emotionally spend the money you want, again and again and again to give the energy outlets into which to flow. You can't say "give me X-amount of dollars and *then* I'll decide what to do with it." Decide what to do with it first; that's the asking that allows the energy to move in. The energy of money needs outlets; no outlets, no money.

- Make a habit of emotionally spending. Observe all sorts of things while you're driving around and start saying, "I'd like that!" "Ooo, I'd like that, too!" "Wow, look at that; that's for me...and that...and that...and that...and that..." while you get into the feeling place of having them. Now you've got Want-momentum going and will find yourself being pulled into circumstances that will either bring the most intense of those desires into your reality, or create openings to allow others to pop in.

- Open to receive! Put those signs all over your house, "OPEN TO RECEIVE!" Place your intent that you are going to lower your resistance to "shoulds and shouldn'ts," and that you're going to learn how to receive. Make it a Want: "I want to learn to receive." Then get over the guilty victim mode that says you're only a good person when you're giving; that's dogmatic hogwash!

- Don't take score too soon. You can't write a script today, and say "where is it" tomorrow.

- Watch your excuses. You'll never pull in the bucks with valve-closing excuses such as "not enough education," "they only hire from the inside," "inept staff," "bad timing," etc. Even if you've got all the "proper" things going for you like education, training, and positioning, none of that will count for squat if you let excuses get in your way.

- If you've got a bunch of negative people in your life right now who are strongly into lack, that's a pretty fair indication of what station you're still tuned into. You might want to take stock.

- Want to measure the amount of negativity in your life? Check the amount of dollars you have coming in. For those of us who have had to struggle with money most of our lives, considerable negativity going out means not many dollars coming in! For us, dollars come or stay away in direct proportion to the negative energy we are—or are not—vibrating.

- And finally, always remember that what has been has nothing whatsoever to do with what can be! If you've had a tough time all your life, you have the tools now to turn that around. If you've not had the sales you'd like to have had, the salary, the recognition, success, the peace, the happiness, and/or overall prosperity you'd like, that is all readily changeable.

How fast? You have only to start flowing differently on a fairly regular basis, and a new world will follow as surely as night follows day. It must. It is cosmic law, the physics of the universe.

relationships and other treasures

Much of this chapter I'd rather forget about, since the subject of intimate relationships relative to deliberate creating is not one to which I can speak personally. My superb résumé encompassing some forty or fifty years of relationships comes from my pre energy-flowing days, and shows it! I was a victim extraordinaire, an unrealistic romantic, a first-class codependent, and a roaring Miss Goody-Two-Shoes. So much for my outstanding track record with relationships.

Be that as it may, I'll pass on the basic tenets of creating meaningful relationships through energy flow, as the process is no different from creating anything. For in truth, anytime we have an alliance, to whatever extent, with any one or any thing, that constitutes a relationship. So here we go.

It Ain't the Dorky Habits

Relationships, be they with a spouse, partner, friend, or business associate, are, like everything else in our world, about how we are vibrating. Period. And how we are vibrating is coming from how we are feeling. Period!

That being the case, it's not going to take a genius to figure out that if we're feeling *anything* other than at peace with ourselves, as well as totally allowing and appreciative of our partner (good luck), our vibrations are going to be slicing away at that relationship, no matter how much we're convinced that since there's nothing wrong with us, it must be the other guy's fault.

If we are verbally or mentally accusing, berating, or disapproving in any way, we are attracting negatively.

If we are feeling trapped, ignored or neglected, unsafe, misunderstood, or short-changed, we are attracting negatively.

If we race in to please, rescue, or placate, we are attracting negatively.

And I can already hear the "Yeah buts":

"Yeah, but you don't know my partner!"

"Yeah, but how would you feel if you had to live with this one or work with that one?"

Now granted, when two people are involved, there are two doing the vibrating, and rarely do those vibrations match. Nonetheless, we are the sole and exclusive creator of our experience, not our partner, not our parents, not even the boss who just got us fired.

So as hard as it may be to swallow, it becomes a matter of looking at *our own* valve, *our own* reactions, *our own* focus, *our own* energy flow, because as long as we're glaring somewhere else—past or present—at all the stuff we don't like, not only are we inviting more of the same, we're blocking all the good things we'd like to see in its place.

The bottom line is, if our partner, or anyone else who classifies as a relationship, has some dorky little habits that annoy us (Don't Wants), and we focus on them with even moderately closed valves, all we're doing is perpetuating the dorky habits we'd like to erase, because we're holding them in our vibration.

And therein lies the cause of every downward spiral of any relationship that ever went sour; the relentless—though surely innocent—attention to disagreeable conditions, no matter how meaningless they may appear to be. As any small, unimportant aggravation begins to snowball into something major from our continued focus and negative energy flow toward it, we'll start to get more of other unpleasant things on that same wavelength, as well as enlarge the petty thing we've been grousing about. That means not only will that infamous toothpaste cap never get put back on the tube, but that very irritation has the potential, with our constant negative focus, to escalate into an unwanted extra-marital affair, a fender bender, a layoff, even a divorce.

"The worse it gets, the worse it gets," remember? A constant flow of annoyance over anything will, sooner or later, turn ugly. It must. Like attracts like.

Sure, when someone is pushing our buttons, every ounce of us wants to push back. But it's never about what we *do* in a relationship that equals what we get. Never! It's not even about how our partner is flowing energy. Like everything else in our world, whatever it is we have in our face has come squarely from how we ourselves have been feeling, flowing, and vibrating.

There's just no other way to put it; if you want to change the conditions of your relationship, you're going to have to change your vibrations.

The Culprit Is Blame

Most of us think of blame as the melodramatic pointing of a long, crooked finger towards one who has done scandalous wrong. Yet we're actually into blame just about every waking moment of our days. From weather, to rude drivers, to toothpaste caps, we blame from sunup 'til sundown and never think a thing about it.

Oh sure, more times than not we're probably justified in our accusations, but so what! There's not an ounce of well-being that can squeak through the low, thick vibration of blame, whether it's justified or not. In fact, the electromagnetic energy of blame is so potently charged as it flows from us to others, it can cause those who are usually fairly dependable to mess up all over the place. And for sure, sending blame-energy to someone who's been nasty, stupid, abusive or drunk only amplifies the condition you'd like to see changed.

Some friends who had their luggage put on a wrong flight were fuming and stewing for hours at their hotel over the inefficiency of the airline. Their important luggage, which had been seen but had now vanished, was so completely lost, no one even knew where to start looking. Finally, my friends realized what they were doing, and switched to appreciating the usually competent employees they'd been berating. Within minutes—*minutes!*—they received the call that the luggage was found and would be delivered within the hour. Prior to their change of attitude, the buckets of angry, blameful energy they were sending out was causing the airline workers to turn a minor incident into a snarled up mess.

A lender to whom I had submitted a loan called to tell me they couldn't find an important original paper I knew I had sent. As I was crabbing over the incompetence of their staff, the phone calls kept getting worse. More stuff missing, more facts not properly documented, more problems, problems, problems. The more I knee-jerked into fuming blame, the more this thing was falling apart right before my eyes. Then I realized what I was doing, switched to appreciation for the normally efficient personnel, and in less than fifteen minutes they called to apologize. Everything was there; the loan had been approved.

A participant in one of my seminars couldn't stop blaming her husband for what she perceived to be the cause of their twins' stuttering. After the seminar she reluctantly agreed to undertake a program of brief hubby-appreciation periods daily. She called about six months later to tell me how difficult that had been at first, but as she got into the swing of it, she learned to catch herself at the onset of a blame bout and get her valve open enough to flow some appreciation to the girls, as well as to her husband. As of the last phone call, both of the girls had nearly returned to normal speech. I don't know what happened to poor hubby.

The point is, the energy of blame always makes a bad situation worse. Always!

Let's say there's a bunch of things in a partnership we don't like, some big, some just trivial little things we might even think we're ignoring. But "little" does not exist, and "little" is usually our biggest problem. If something is big enough for us to label, even if that label is "little," there's no way we can say we're ignoring it or accepting it. We're focusing on the bloody thing, so obviously, we're flowing energy to it and making it bigger.

The bottom line is that if we're bothered by something, whether our being bothered is justified or not, we're attracting negatively; that's the way of it! It may be only a mild annoyance over clothes hung backwards. Or it may be as terrible as the fear of abuse. But regardless of the emotional intensity, that negative attention to "what is" will always cause even greater problems, because that's the script we're writing.

True, we can't paint on another's canvas if they don't want it painted on. If someone doesn't want to change, writing a new script or appreciating probably won't accomplish much except get our own valve open. In fact, once we're flowing that kind of energy, the strong possibility exists that the other guy may buck like a spurred yearling and not want any part of whatever it is we're offering, which could well mean we might be looking at a pulling apart.

That's magnetics. If you're with someone who strongly desires not to change, and you do, universal physics will probably split you up and keep you that way. Yes, that may sound fearful, but ask yourself why you'd want to stay with someone who creates their life through negative energy flow?

So never mind your partner's valve. In fact, never mind your partner! Take your focus off of what's going on around you and insist to yourself that you get your own valve open any way you can, no matter what. *NO MATTER WHAT!*

The only way you'll ever have a relationship the way you'd like it to be is to script it that way and stay with that script until it comes about, either with this partner or another with whom you're in greater vibrational harmony (which means, if you haven't already guessed, being a whole lot happier).

We Get to Choose

If you're a silent sufferer, as I was, good luck. Whatever it is you're suffering over is growing like an overfed weed. Same thing if you're a controller, nagger, worrier, or people-pleaser. You have to take your relationship-killing focus OFF whatever it is that's closing your valve and put it ON to what you want in life. In other words, take your focus off your Don't Wants, put it on your Wants and keep it there.

If you've got a drunk on your hands, open your valve and write your new script.

If you've got an unemployed partner on your hands, open your valve and write your new script.

If the two of you are fighting over money, open your valve and write your new script.

Start talking with your partner about what you want and why, not what you don't want and why.

I know, I'm sounding very cavalier about this, like there was nothing to this business of ignoring the actions of some jackass who you're sure is responsible for making your life miserable. Blame is our game, and pointing the finger back on ourselves has always seemed so pointless.

In the middle of writing this chapter I took a break to go do some grocery shopping and maybe go to the steambath to clear my head. I wanted to leave the subject behind for a while to make sure I was touching all bases. Leave it behind? Oh sure!

As I was driving to the store, I started a rather nasty inner dialogue with the folks who were renting the little house on my property. They had been unable to pay the rent for a couple of months, and my focus on that non-payment was becoming all-consuming, to say the least. And anyhow, the car was a great place to fume, so I was going on and on with all these phony undertones of compassion and understanding. Frankly, I was boiling, yet totally oblivious to what I was creating with my vibrations. And here I am writing about it, for Pete's sake!

Fortunately, it was my cantankerous mood in the supermarket that woke me up. Just as I reached for the dog food, it dawned on me how snarly I felt. I asked myself "What's bothering me?" and in an instant realized it was my focus on the lackful conditions of my tenants.

At first I was annoyed at myself, then even more annoyed that I didn't feel like getting out of my mood. I finished my shopping and headed straight for the steamroom, easing myself bit my mit into a better mood as I drove, so that by the time I hit the steam, I was ready to write a new script.

First, a little appreciation: "Nice kids, pleasant to have around." Not exactly rah rah, but better than where I had been. I could feel my resistance simmering down...a little.

"Thank goodness they were there to take care of the dogs while I was away. No other tenants have ever done that. And no other tenants have ever offered to help with the annual house painting touch-up like they did." That felt better.

"And they really do love their place, and have it fixed so cute." By now, my valve was open enough for me to start the new script, so I headed for the empty pool where I could quietly talk out loud without being stared at.

"You both just got new jobs? Wow! That's fantastic! I'm truly happy for you. I know you've been wanting to buy some new furniture, so now you'll be able to do that."

On and on I went, painting the picture I wanted, backing off when I'd go too far and it didn't feel comfortable, pushing ahead when it felt good.

It wasn't ten minutes after I got home that the kids came over beaming from ear to ear. Not a new permanent job yet, but they had found an ongoing means to pay me, starting immediately! Fast action, to say the least!

Though they had been abundantly aware of their inability to pay me, their primary focus was on their love of the place and all the ways they intended to fix it up, not on their lack of money, so we had a vibrational match—theirs and mine. If they had been focused fearfully, all the appreciation in the world wouldn't have made a bit of difference.

Vibrational Ping-Pong

One of my first jobs after I got out of college was in New York City working for what was, at that time, the largest catalog photography house in the world. They did all the fashion shots and most of the still-life photos for Sears and Montgomery Ward.

The best part of my job was working with the stylists, the gals who had to make sure the clothes fit just right by stuffing everything from rolling pins to beer cans in all the right places. Day in and day out the top male and female models of the day whizzed through our studios. I didn't pay much attention to them, but there was one striking, tall willowy redhead who seemed to be the constant butt of everyone's jokes. Each time she'd breeze in, by the time she was ready to leave, a whole new round of wisecracks were circulating through the office before she was out the door.

It seems this gal had a revolving boyfriend problem, so revolving that each time she showed up for a shoot, which was several times a week, she'd either be wailing about the last one or in ecstasy over the new one. She was like a ping pong ball, breaking up every time the ball crossed the net.

"That bastard! He wouldn't return one of my calls. He's just like all the rest, so engrossed in his own petty world, he has no time for mine. He seems to have time for his other girlfriends, though."

All she could do was blame, blame, blame and attract so many more clones, so fast, it became the standing corporate joke. Off and on someone felt a twinge of compassion and said something like, "How can such a beautiful girl like that have such a string of bad luck? With all she's got going for her, how could that happen?"

String of bad luck? No. This beautiful young woman was attracting from her old vibrational script, her old habitual way of viewing men. Her script never changed. She knew she could attract men like bees to honey, and indeed she did, but they all ended up being the same kind, attracted by what she was continually vibrating. As each poor clone would turn up, only to pass into extinction, she'd flow out yet another litany of negative Don't Wants to attract the next one, and the next and the next. Since her dominant vibration regarding her string of ex-boyfriends was always "that rotten person," that's all she ever attracted: "rotten person" replicas. The blame she held in her memories sent out such powerfully magnetized vibrations, there was never a chance for a different kind of relationship to activate.

To Forgive Is To What?

First comes blame, and then comes what...forgiveness? Maybe. Maybe not.

It goes without saying that the exalted position of forgiveness can come about only after one has first convicted. Which means the way we usually look at forgiveness is not much different than blame. Which means we rarely, genuinely, forgive.

Something happens, somebody says something, and then like the trained seals we are, we vibrationally bark

217

back. If we'd let it go at that, we'd be in great shape. But we continue to allow our negative emotions to spill out all over the place, and BHAM! We're into the blame mode.

But now let's say that we've decided to forgive somebody. How nice. Here's the flash: Forgiveness is a releasing of *our* resistance to positive energy, not the transgressor's at whom we are so benevolently aiming our forgiving smile. Forgiveness is about forgetting the thing ever happened in the first damn place. *Ho HO!!!!*

Usually when we forgive, we are acknowledging that whomever we're forgiving has done a wrong, which is probably true. Then, even though we say we forgive, we secretly hold on to the dastardliness of the wrong. Yet true forgiveness is about no longer holding onto or stewing over (focusing on) the thing that got us all riled up to begin with. And that holds true whether it happened five minutes or fifty years ago. Why? Because unless we let it go, we'll keep getting more of it, that's why. If we hold on to it, it's in our vibration. And if it's in our vibration, we're either going to attract it, or something similar in vibration. Over and over and over.

If there's a need to forgive, there had to be judgment or blame precede that need, otherwise there'd be no reason to forgive. And judgment or blame means we're focusing on a Don't Want. So the first step in forgiving (and you're probably not going to like this) is releasing the resistance that caused the blame in the first place, meaning the ability to say...and mean, "Who cares!? Who gives a hoot!? Maybe the idiot did do something awful, something really tasteless. So what!?"

218

What we're talking about now is honest-to-God unconditional love, something I'm sure not one in fifty million of us has ever understood. I didn't. I always thought unconditional love meant you loved somebody in spite of what a degenerate they were, which of course meant I was still focusing on their degenerateness, holding it in my own vibration.

What unconditional love really means is:

"I will keep my valve open to well-being no matter what crazy thing you've done." (Remember, you don't have to change it or even like it; you just have to stop focusing on it!)

It means "I don't need conditions to be just right to be happy. I'm not going to pay any more attention to your silly habits, because I don't need everything to be perfect for my love to flow to you."

"You can be nasty, you can say mean hurtful things, but your choice does not affect my choice, which is to keep my valve open and feel good. I am no longer blaming any negative conditions and/or your negative habits for the way I feel!!!"

Sure, I know that sounds nearly impossible, but what's it going to take for us to allow happiness? The neat thing about getting into this space of "I don't give a hoot what you do or did, my valve is staying open any-how" is that you are automatically allowing the kind of conditions to come in that *you want*—definitely the name of the game. You are no longer hinging how you experience life on the actions of others.

Am I saying to forgive an abuser? No, not in the old sense, never. To forgive in the old, normal way means you're still holding the wrong in your vibration and inviting more of the same. I'm saying forget it, get your own valve open, write a new script, and vibrate your way out of that mess.

Am I saying to forgive an adulterer? No, not in the old way. If the agreement between the two of you is monogamy, I'm saying forget it and get your own valve open if you don't want it repeated in this relationship or the next. Either you're going to vibrationally pull in the harmony you desire, or a new mate.

So am I saying, "Don't forgive"? Good gravy no. On the contrary, I'm saying forgive at the drop of a hat. "Do I forgive you? Of course, now what's next?" That's a long, long way from, "Well I don't know, Honey, that was a pretty awful thing you did."

Even a little bit of forgiving at a time will work, then a little more, and a little more if that's the only way you can do it. But one thing's for sure; unless you want more of the same, forgiving ultimately means forgetting!

The plain fact is, focusing on what you don't want in a relationship is never going to get you what you want. Never in a billion years. For a relationship to change to your liking, it's gotta be:

Focus *off* the condition;

Focus *onto* opening the valve...yours.

That's the only way your unwanted conditions are ever going to change, and the only way your relationship will survive.

"How Can I Help?"

"I have a mate who is disabled. How can I help him?"

"I have a mate out of work. What can I do to help?"

"I have a brother who is angry at the world. Is there anything I can do?"

We all want to help. We want to give, or do, or say something that will make it better for someone.

But take care; a helping hand is not always what it appears to be.

If you'll think about those questions for a minute, you'll see the focus is squarely on the other guy. And when it's on the other guy's pain, you're joining with that vibration, merging it with your own until your valve becomes as closed as theirs. Your focus is on the negative condition, which is giving you more negative feelings than you had to begin with. And even worse, you're helping your friend to more negativity than they had before you joined up with them vibrationally.

So how do you help? The first thing to do is get into a good feeling place and get your own valve open before you do any thinking about the person. Then you can inspire—not insure, just inspire—that same valve openness in the person you're thinking about. You're no longer attempting to paint on their canvas, but you're genuinely offering them paints and brushes.

On the other hand, if you keep thinking about how awful it is that your someone has cancer, or is out of a job, or just had their house burn down, that lackful vibration stands to reinforce the lackful vibration they're already in.

221

Instead, as you think about them, see them the way you want them to be. If there's anything within them wanting to move forward, your bursts of positive, loving energy will have a strong influence on their thinking, feeling, and being.

That's why prayers for the sick so rarely work. When we see the one for whom the prayer is being offered as being deficient in some way, we're coming from a place of lack. We are viewing that person as deficient in some way, when in fact they are every bit as adequate as any power in the universe. They've just forgotten; and for a time, so did those of us doing the praying.

I have a friend whose father was dying of an empty life 3000 miles away on the opposite coast. Every night as she went to sleep she would send her father healing thoughts, hoping to help him come around. But in her own saddened state, she was seeing him in his lack, alone and melancholy, a pathetic picture of a man without friends, without incentive, without the will to live. He kept getting worse.

Then she got wind of the Law of Attraction and realized she had been doing exactly the opposite of what had been her intent. After that, as she lay in bed each night, she would see her dad as he used to be: vital, filled with fun, spirited, gregarious. She refelt the wonderful times they had playing tennis together and the merriment of the family ice skating on the local pond. She could feel herself just melt into the joy of those feelings and times. Within three days—*three days!*—her dad called saying he felt better than he had felt in years, and would it be okay if he came out for a visit!

Was she responsible for this change? Only in providing her dad with an opportunity to pick up these new paints and brushes. She had given him a vibrational leg up, much like we might toss a life-jacket to someone. They can grab it or not; but the choice is theirs, and theirs alone.

Breaking Up

"Should I—shouldn't I? Should I—shouldn't I?" We've all gone through it, that disturbing period when we know it's time to do something, but the answers just don't seem to come. Or we don't want to get them.

If you've been exploring the ins and outs of deliberate creating with the Law of Attraction, and your mate hasn't, you may be in for a little pulling apart unless good old mate decides to come along. If you've offered paints and brushes 'til you're purple, with no response, then you might be in for some pulling apart. Or maybe you're ready to pull apart anyhow. Either way, let's take a look at some new ways to consider this breaking up scene.

First off, we've got another one of those emotionally charged words to deal with. This time it's "relationship." Not real high on most people's Feel Good lists, that's for sure. Just thinking of that word packs almost as much negative wallop as "money." Maybe it started with our own family, or maybe just with our own troublesome partnerships, or both. It doesn't matter. The very word "relationship" evokes a mixed bag of longings and shivers in the same breath.

So it stands to reason (pre-becoming a deliberate creator) that when we break up, or are faced with that possibility, or even if we've already done it, the thought of getting into a new tangled web is not always enticing. And yet, that's what we do, get right back into another twosome with the same script or worse. Only the players have changed.

We gotta change the script! If we want it different, either now or with the next relationship, we gotta see it and feel it to be different. If we want it different, *we gotta change the script.*

Let's say you're out of it now, living by yourself. You're enjoying this deliberate creating routine, and so you decide you're ready for a venture with a new partner. But what's the first thing you think about? The old one!!!! And nine times out of ten, that thinking comes packed with some heavy negative vibrations. Just like the attractive model who couldn't get the kind of guy she wanted, you become locked right back into attracting a clone of the last one, or worse.

You have to change the script and get those vibrations you're holding onto...OUT!! You have to manufacture, somehow, a revised feeling about your ex. If you don't, if you keep holding on for dear life to the resentments, angers and peeves, your next go-around can't help but be the same sort of thing or worse, because that's the vibration you're putting out: resentments, angers, and peeves. What you vibrate is what you get. You can't vibrate with thoughts of "back there" and expect to get something totally different "up here."

This might not be thrilling news to you, but relationships never die. They never cease. Just by virtue of the two of you (or three of you or twenty of you) having been together in a house, or an office, or a club, you have a vibrational tie that never, never stops. So if you let any one of those ties remain negative...well, you know the rest. That vibration will be forever radiating out from you, looking for its match.

Maybe you lived with a physical abuser, or maybe just a jerk. If you don't want more of the same, you have to find something to love about that blockhead, something you can appreciate to let you break the negative vibrational ties. Otherwise, no matter how long you wait between partners, and no matter how much so-called healing you think you've done, you'll be pulling in the same junky things you didn't like about your ex, because you're still focused on them, grumbling over them, telling friends how glad you are to be rid of them, not to mention being mad at yourself for putting up with them for so long. If you're thinking about it, and feeling it, you're still vibrating it, so you *will* attract it.

Same thing with blameful focus on our parents. We get what we focus on, pure and simple, so it's an odds-on bet that if you had ugly stuff in your childhood that you're still hanging on to, you're a shoo-in to attract it in some kind of relationship, whether in marriage, with neighbors, or at work.

But back to your current situation. Let's say you're still involved with the relationship, still living or working together with a question as to whether you should or shouldn't remain. Now is the time to take your focus off the conditions, ask yourself what's been bothering you, and start getting those negative vibrations reversed. That may or may not make a difference in your present relationship, but it will definitely take your focus off the problem so you can get some answers, for you can only get answers (inspiration, ideas, etc.) when you unhook your focus from the problem and move to a higher frequency.

So love 'em, whether or not they were or are lovable. Appreciate them, no matter how justified you may be in sticking pins in their voodoo doll. Break the chain of negative attraction, then you can find your answers as to leaving or staying. And if you do leave, you won't be attracting a clone on the same old negative wavelength.

Chain of Pain

I had a long-time friend who would call every other month or so from several states away and dump all of her rather robust problems on me. Most of this was before I knew about getting sucked into—and pulled down with—someone else's negative vibrations.

This routine went on for years, an unending diatribe of the same old problems growing bigger and bigger as time went on.

At each phone call, I'd jump right in to join her in her negative feelings, thinking I was being so helpful. I'd empathize, commiserate, sympathize, until I'd feel so bad, I'd have to go outside for a walk-about in nature to get my balance back after hanging up.

Without knowing it, not only was I fanning her negativity, but I was wrapping it tightly around me! It was awful, and I didn't know how to stop it short of telling her not to call any more, which I didn't have the heart to do. To make matters worse, even when I wasn't talking to her on the phone, I'd be envisioning her in her messes, surrounded by lack, a walking time bomb waiting to explode into another tangled predicament.

When I finally got the picture of what I was doing vibrationally to both of us, I started sending different kinds of thoughts to her, seeing her in abundance, happiness, gaiety, etc., though frankly, it wasn't easy. But she didn't want out of her misery, and she surely didn't want anything to do with my paint and brushes.

Finally one day she called and read me the riot act for not going along with her thinking, calling me callous, heartless, self-centered, and a few more colorful jewels I won't bother to repeat. In a manner of speaking, she was probably right, since I was no longer willing to join in her Chain of Pain. I had to let her sink, or I'd go down with her again, something I was no longer willing to do. I've never heard from her since, but continue to see her in the best script I can muster. Perhaps one day...

Try as we will, fix-it kits don't work. When we decide someone needs fixing (as I was doing with my friend), all we're doing is viewing them as "wrong," flooding them with negative energy.

Instead, if we can find something—*anything*—to appreciate about them, and plant the seeds of potential new growth about them with our positive vibrations, we open up a chance for change.

If you want to help someone out of their immediate suffering, sending a simple "It's going to be all right" will usually quiet them down and give them an opportunity for a moment of Feel Good. As Pollyannaish as that might sound, it's a soother for them, and a respite for you. Now they're in a place to accept your paint and brushes, or not. If they choose not, so be it. But joining them, even in heartfelt compassion, will only compound the misery by magnifying the negative vibrations: theirs *and* yours.

Every person on this planet has the Guidance within to find their own way, if they so choose. But sometimes we have to let them sink if that's their choice, or we'll go down too, connected vibrationally in the Chain of Pain.

Families and Harmony?

If someone in your family is driving you nuts, not only is your focus making it worse, it's affecting every other area of your life. A closed valve over a problem youngster is a closed valve to all of Life. A closed valve over a mate is a closed valve to Life. So, how can we get people under one roof going in somewhat the same direction, even if on different tracks? Here's what a close friend did with remarkable success.

Without going into details, the teenage son was acting as the catalyst for everybody's ugly feelings. The whole family was being painfully torn apart with his drug-related antics.

As Peg, his mother and my friend, started getting more and more into the Law of Attraction, she decided to see if everybody could amalgamate their individual intents into a more focused direction, rather than spraying them all over the place. They all had a hard time at first, because everybody was keeping their Don't Want focus on the son, rather than on their own valve.

Nonetheless, they started having family meetings to voice their Wants. As might be expected, the first few go-arounds emerged as long lists of Don't Wants from everyone, particularly from the son. But after a while— quite a while—everybody was stating their positive Wants openly and enthusiastically.

The next step was to get into the Whys. Home run! As soon as they did that, the true colors of desire began to fly. All anybody wanted was to feel better than they were currently feeling, so that became their joint intent. From there, miracles began to pop.

For the first time ever, they all truly wanted to be together, to do things together, go places together; they wanted to feel like a family. It was working! Although son's grades didn't exactly fly off the card, he turned around enough to stay in school, while both mom and pop stayed pretty much off his back. And, since both mom and pop were determined to keep their own valves open and see their son as a spirited, happy young man, they vibrationally merged with the son's underlying intent, so that the drugs eventually vanished without intervention.

Peg and her family didn't sail off into the sunset, not by a long shot. They continued getting caught up in the old habits of needing conditions to change before they could be happy. But they were a committed lot, and kept at their weekly family get-togethers to restate their intents and Wants. Whenever circumstances got rough again with any one member, the others found they could maintain their own connectedness enough to help both themselves and the other guy until all were reconnected again to their Source energy and back on their own open-valve tracks.

No Matter What, *No Matter What*

Like everything else, when we stop getting lost in the conditions and start dealing with our own valve, life takes on a new glow. If we would look for ways to appreciate and praise, rather than to criticize and blame, we can be the essential catalyst that helps tip the scales up to positive attracting for everybody, including ourselves.

Keep a watchful eye out for valve-closing statements like "I love you, but..." or "Why don't you ever..."

Look instead for valve-*opening* statements such as "I don't know how it's going to turn out for you, but I know it's going to be fine." "I never worry about you, I never worry about us, because I know whatever is in store will be good." If ever there was a time and place to work on Positive Aspects, family is it!

And there's another plus to appreciating family folk; once your valve is swinging open, it's swinging open to everything, not just family. You can be appreciating your mate of present or past, and your new job will happen! You can be a single parent appreciating your children, and your new mate will happen! You can be appreciating your home, and your problem kids will turn around!

It's all energy, it's all vibration stemming from how you're feeling. So write your new script, don't worry about the whens or hows, give up noticing it hasn't happened yet, get your eyes off of the other guy's valve, and find ways to open yours. Before you know it, it won't matter what anyone else in your house or on the planet is doing, because you are no longer a responder; you are now an aware creator.

Just open your own valve no matter what, no matter what, *NO MATTER WHAT!* The rest will take care of itself. Another guarantee.

living
the body,
dying the body

I hope I've made it quite clear by now that I'm not yet walking on water, manifesting gold coins in my hand, or maintaining half a dozen resort villas to which I flee in one of my four Lamborghinis when I tire of my servant-laden estates overlooking the Caribbean.

Has my life changed since learning to direct my energy flow? Like an about face! Sure, I still have an ample supply of old beliefs that cause my teeter-tottering scales to tip toward negative focus, negative feelings, a closed valve and bad moods...until I catch 'em and turn 'em around. Sometimes the process is fast and electrifying; other times so slow it seems like lifetimes pass before I get myself talked out of a downer.

There is, however, one area of my recent energy-flowing life that has been more of a joy to me than the freedom of money or any of the other betterments of well-being, and that is my body.

When I was in my forties, in the midst of my worst victimhood years, I had one lousy bad back. Sometimes I couldn't get out of bed for a week. Other times the spasms that grabbed me were so intensely painful, I'd let out screams that could be heard in the next state. Although I'd manage to scrunch into the car, I'd finally make it to work, only to stand or kneel all day at my desk, as sitting was far too painful.

No sooner did I begin to get that mess under control with a stringent exercise routine, than I was off to visit four hundred twenty-two and a half different doctors to find out why my heart was doing the rhumba all day instead of a quiet two-step. A holistic M.D. finally labeled it severe hypoglycemia (low blood sugar), "probably brought on by stress." A slight understatement.

I was not in good shape emotionally, physically, mentally, or spiritually. I already put well over two decades of Alcoholics Anonymous under my belt, but nothing was working except that I was sober; I couldn't have found a spiritual direction if my life depended on it, which at that point, it did. I was in big trouble.

Then it was joints that didn't want to move, excess weight, lack of energy, poor eyesight, bad teeth, and hair going bye-bye; all sure signs of...signs of what? Normal aging? No, all sure signs of a life being lived with a valve more closed than open, a life being lived more disconnected to my Source energy than connected, a life projecting far more negative vibrations than positive. Which is all that aging is anyhow.

But why had I shut down so? Where was all the negativity coming from that had become so destructive to my body? I wasn't a nasty ogre or a cruel wicked person wearing my negativity on my sleeve. Actually, I had grown up as a ordinary kid from an ordinary upper middle class dysfunctional family. I had done all the right things, gone to the right colleges, worn the right clothes, held the right jobs and lived in the right places, all with an unfailing pleasantness to my demeanor and properly timed smiles on my face. Yet that underlying tone of "normal" negativity was my constant companion, and the older I got, the more it blossomed.

Sometimes I had fun. Sometimes I was happy. Never in a million years, though, did I consider myself to be negative, and neither did my friends. On the contrary, I was viewed as the embodiment of optimistic cheer. Still, I was always worried—about everything. With a grin on my face and a good word always on my lips, my constant focus was on lack—in either myself or others. Just like everybody else I knew.

Now, more than twenty years after the back and low blood sugar episodes, and several years of working with the Law of Attraction, I've never looked better, felt better, moved better, or been better. Not even when I was in my teens did I have this kind of stamina, and I'd have to go back to some other lifetime that I'm surely not aware of to dig up this kind of passion for life and living.

Fear is rarely a visitor to my world, not even worry or concern. Money comes easily, most of the time. (You thought I was a pro at this? Surely you jest!) New ideas abound. Work is accomplished with fun and ease. I'm doing what I want to do, when I want to do it... for the most part. Bouts of negative focus last only briefly, or for as long as I feel like having them. A continuum of days that are extraordinarily happy comes by my design. And the by-product to all of this? Ah, my astoundingly good health!

Our Crucial Lifeline

These days just about everybody knows that the state of one's physical health is connected to the state of one's mental health. Even doctors, by crackie! Scientists stress the hell out of mice, then watch the cancer cells develop. They deprive baby chimps of mama's breast, and watch them develop diabetes. The whole scientific/medical community knows all too well there's some kind of link between body and mind, they're just not sure what it is...yet. Won't they be surprised when they find out it's nothing but our own energy.

(I can see the cartoon now: Two doctors standing opposite each other over an opened-up patient on the operating table. One says to the other, "I've got the tumor out, but where's that damn valve we're supposed to open?")

Illness in any form is nothing more than our negative energies choking off so much of our Life flow—those higher frequencies that are our natural state—that cellular damage results.

Oh sure, we're always attached energetically by at least a string of that Life force, or we'd be outta here. But a pinched-up string (closed valve), and a wide open Feel Good valve which allows that Life force energy to flow through us freely, are two very different things. One starves the body of its natural Life force and Life-giving energy, while the other feeds the body. It follows, then, that if a state of higher-than-usual vibration is maintained on a fairly regular basis, sickness cannot possibly happen or be maintained. It just can't.

The body, after all, isn't separate from the universe, so when we think a thought, the vibrations run through the body as well as everywhere else. If those vibrations are in harmony with our body's intrinsic programming for well-being (open valve Feel Good), then the cells thrive.

But if it's negative energy we're projecting, the cells can't remain strong enough to do their job. All they've had to feed on are the physical foods we've ingested, and that's simply not enough to keep them going. Without the high frequency energy of Life force necessary for them to survive, they eventually weaken and die before their time, no longer able to replicate normally and sustain healthy life.

Illness exists for only one reason: someone has flowed more low frequency energy than high. Which, of course, is why so much illness exists. Find the generally happy person, the one who constantly pulls themselves up and out of negative emotions, and you'll find a healthy person. Always! People who are sick have shut themselves off in some degree from their Lifeline. It may not be so obvious on the outside, but in some way or other, they've closed their valve off to their Source energy through worry, blame, guilt, whatever.

Sick people are just misinformed, like all of us. They can be devoutly religious, honest, upstanding citizens, dear and trusted friends, but if they are not allowing enough of the flow of their own greater energy into their lives, they are not allowing Life. Indeed, all illness, without exception, is the disallowance of that higher energy flow, and the ultimate manifestation of one's endless negative emotion.

If You're Ill

If you currently have an illness, then right off the bat I'll recommend you stay with your doctor, stay with your treatment, stay with whatever your recovery program is, as that is undoubtedly where your beliefs lie. No sense in ruffling the waters until some new beliefs and new vibrational changes are strongly in place.

For centuries we've held to the doctrine that only something outside of ourselves could make us better, so until we learn to override that gargantuan belief, only an activity which resonates with that conviction—e.g., continuing to go outside of self for medical assistance—can possibly offer any measure of recovery. That recovery may be minimal or shaky at best, for if the thoughts and energy flows don't change, the original illness or something worse will be back. But for now, stay with your doctor!

However, if you are sick, I ask you to know from the depths of your being that any illness is reversible. While there is probably no more difficult task in this world than attempting to feel up when you're physically down, it is not only achievable, it has been done many, many times.

Norman Cousins did it, the publisher who was dying of cancer. He declared "No way am I checking out" and decided to spend his time in a state of laughter. He knew instinctively that if he could reverse the frequencies in his body, it would heal itself. So from his hospital bed he watched only funny movies, read funny books, had friends tell him jokes, and cured himself completely of the cancer that had raked his body. Then he wrote a book about it. I have to hand it to him; that is one committed soul...and teacher.

Cousin's recovery is a prime example of what we're talking about here, that it's not our genes, not our sexual habits, not our ingestion of bad meats, and not even our exposure to infection that is at the core of our illness. A connected person flowing Life force energy through their body can never, ever, be affected by those things. What causes illness is body-starving, the disallowance of Life Source energy so critical to health and well-being.

Now obviously, the most spontaneous thing we do when hit with an illness, particularly one we view as serious, is fly into action, rush to a doctor, and never take our thoughts off the condition. We're frightened, so of course that's how we react. And yet with our constant negative focus on the illness, we're cutting off the most important ingredient available to reverse the condition: the curative powers of our higher frequencies.

Mild Cooking/Hefty Cooking

No illness or accident happens overnight. Adversities take a while to cook, usually several years. While your more-down-than-up energy over the years is indeed the hard-to-swallow cause of what you may be looking at right now, that has not one thing in this world to do with what can be!

If, for instance, you've been in a serious accident, it didn't happen all of a sudden out of nowhere. As you look back over the years, could you say your pattern of thought has leaned just a little toward low frequencies: anger at family, ticked off at circumstances, aching to be liked, fear of failure, blame, concern over finances, hidden guilt over whatever? *It would have to be so, or you would not have had the accident.* That negative momentum builds over time, and builds and builds until finally you step into your self-made vortex with another who has his tuning fork pitched the same as yours. And you come together, often head on.

Low frequency energy is the cause; body damage—either accident or illness—is the effect whether it's been building for a few weeks or several decades.

And then there's the matter of intensity. Mild, lukewarm negativity over a period of years is still negative vibration, and your body responds in kind with a mild, lukewarm problem. By the same token, a hefty negative flowing of your energy over the years (or months) will yield a hefty illness or a good-sized accident.

But whatever the physical problem may be, it is nothing more than the result of vibrational abuse to the body, a result which can be undone far more rapidly than it took to create.

Fooling the Grownup

To turn an illness around, once again we go for trickery, looking for ways to trick the mind into creating the high vibrations required for the cells to begin their process of regeneration. This is not a cure-all; nothing is, for only a change in energy across the board will bring that transformation about. This is a beginning, and one that can work wonders.

This trickery is much like writing a new script, but with some important twists added to unhinge a veritable storehouse of rusted old beliefs. We're going to play a little kid's game called "Let's Pretend," and I promise, if you will dive into this wholeheartedly and play the game full throttle, your valve *will* open. Okay, here's part one.

Let's Pretend, Part One: "What If..."

First, get the jump-start smile on your face, then move into a buzz from that Gentle Inner Smile. When you've got that going, reach back in time to the little kid in you, because the game we're going to play is the game of "What If."

"What would I do if..."

"Where would I go if..."

"How would I play if..." If what?!

...if you were healthy as a horse!

...if you were young, and strikingly good looking!

...if you were the frisky, frolicsome youngster you used to be or always wanted to be!

...if you had three wishes and could do anything you wanted to do, and have anything you wanted to have.

Get into it and live it as much as you can until the *feeeelings* of fun and excitement flood through you. (If you're feeling foolish, that's a pretty fair indication of how stuck you are in rigid adult—meaning generally negative—vibrations.)

Let's Pretend, Part Two: "Back Then"

Now call to mind (and feeling) some actual times when you truly were vibrantly healthy and happy, and the buoyant feelings that went with those times.

Maybe it was playing hockey after school on a frozen pond, or cheerleading in high school. Maybe it was meandering along a lazy summer stream picking watercress, or bobsledding with friends down the back nine of the golf course, or hayriding with your first love under a harvest moon. Whatever it was, find your times and go back to the happy feelings that went with them.

Let's Pretend, Part Three: "Blending Together"

And now, put both together. Bounce back and forth between the two feelings, gradually merging your "What Ifs" and your "Back Thens" into one feeling tone. Let them flow together in a symphony of happy vibrations until the sunny feelings of "Back Then" overlay onto the desired outcomes of "What If." They become one feeling, one happiness, one joyful remembrance. Most important, *they are now one outcome!*

You can't look at how much you don't want your illness, and expect to open your valve to well-being at the same time, any more than you can look at not having enough money and feel good about it. It's got to be one or the other, open valve or closed. Feel good and allow the Life force to flow through you to wellness; or be scared stiff, cut off the Life flow, and perpetuate the illness. Cancer has never been the cause of death to the body, but cutting off the Life force through fear, anger, blame, or any other negative vibration will do it every time.

If you will allow yourself to really get into playing "What If" and "Back Then" and stop being such a stuffy grownup, you *will* reach the feelings required to begin bodily changes. The moment you do, the moment you *feeeeel* yourself as healthy as you used to be or want to be, *and can feel it throughout the depths of your being,* you launch a whole new creation of you out into time that now exists in a vortex of thought as surely as a tree stands in the forest. You may not be in the forest to see the tree, but it's there. You know it's there; now don't ignore it.

Go often to that place of thought to check out the looks of this new body you've created. Take with you the feelings merged from your games. With those buoyant feelings in place, slip into your new body to check out its shape, how it fits, how it feels, how it works, even how it smells. Pretend, pretend, and *feeeeel.*

If you're in pain, wait for a time when the pain has lessened, then step into the healing world of "Let's Pretend." Go there as often as you can. Then get out of your own way, meaning keep your focus off of what hasn't happened yet, and let the universe do its thing.

Change the Look

At a talk I gave recently I was asked (as I almost always am) how to get to that feeling place of "thin," when you can see quite clearly that you're fat. It was another "Let's Pretend" scenario, knowing that you can't think thin—much less get there—when you're feeling fat.

A gal in the back, who was frantically waving her hand, spoke up with the kind of excitement I usually associate with winning the lottery. I mean, she had something to say in no uncertain terms, and sure enough, she hit the nail on the head.

It seems this gal had wanted to lose a considerable amount of weight, went through all the usual diets, lost, put back on, lost, put back on, as we've all done. Finally she got into visualization which sounded liked a good idea, but went nowhere until she decided to put some emotional pizzazz behind the imagery. Then all sorts of things started happening.

First came her idea to work out at the gym. A good start, but she was astonished to find she couldn't even fake a desire to go to the gym if she was allowing herself to feel fat! Even more important, she found that as long as she was focusing on her weight, any notion of sticking with a diet, past the first few pounds, went out the window.

So back she went into the visualizations and pretending games where, at first, she had to almost bully herself into *feeeeeling* the weight she wanted to be. It worked. As long as she continued to pretend thin, and feel thin, and keep her focus off of feeling fat, she could maintain her not-too-stringent diet with relative ease, and no longer had to fight with herself about going to the gym. I don't know what her weight was before, but this lovely young woman was a picture-perfect size twelve when I saw her.

This is not just simple "wanting" to be thin or well. You can't just want and expect it to happen. It's refocusing and refeeling, refocusing and refeeling, refocusing and refeeling. Your body will always respond to the image you give it, provided it's accompanied with the appropriate feeling; fat or thin, sick or well.

The secret to reversing anything within the body is to get your focus off what you don't want, find any way you can to get into that feeling-place of what you do want, then know with a certainty that the laws of the universe are working and must bring that felt vision into reality, as long as you don't squelch it.

What's Wrong Is Never Right

There is truly no sense in staying away from doctors if your beliefs say doctors work. While I've turned the health and shape of my body around dramatically, I know what my mind will and will not allow right now, so I still make an occasional visit to an MD or dentist.

But think about it for a minute. What are doctors trained to do? Heal you? Sure, that's the objective, as soon as they find out what's *wrong* with you.

"What's wrong" is their business, their reason for being. Yes, they want to help, but if they don't find something wrong, how can they help you? Since "what's wrong" is what they're looking for—and what you expect them to find—that is precisely what they—and you—are going to attract: something that is wrong.

Haven't you noticed that with doctors we're either on the verge of getting something, or we've got one foot in the grave? We're either precancerous or haven't a chance. I'm not knocking those in the medical profession; they're a grand and commendable group just now

245

beginning to understand the process of wellness. But we don't have to join them in attracting any more of what we want to get rid of, and we certainly don't have to visit them in fear with closed valves.

If you've been told you're in some sort of "pre" condition, and it's scaring the pants off you, slow down and take a look at what you're creating. You've closed your valve by becoming fearful, you're magnetizing negatively, and are now headed straight toward the inevitable fulfillment of the doctor's verdict. Every doctor on the face of this planet knows that illness soars once the diagnosis is given. Fancy that!

By all means go to your doctor, but watch your reactions, your fears, your beliefs, your denial—which means watch your valve. Set the so-called incurable rate aside, along with any other gruesome statistics about the disease. This way you can employ your doctor as a means to the end you desire, rather than as a cause for any further fear.

Death Is a Joke

We've been talking a lot about the pure positive energy that creates worlds, the energy to which we are always connected but rarely open. Since our body is an extension of that primal force of Life, why do we die?

Let's say you're an actor. You get on stage, put on a costume, and experience the fun of being a character in the play. When you're done, you put the costume and character aside, but you're still you.

Same thing with your Expanded Self. It's here playing around in a body (yours) for the sheer experience of it all, for the learning, for the fun. When it tires of this, it will do something else, but it won't go out like a candle. It can't; it's pure energy, and you can't snuff out energy.

Ah, but even though energy can't be squelched, our negative vibrations most surely can squelch physical cells, a practice we seem to sanction with an appalling vitality. Focus with fear on a condition in the body we don't want, and our link to the greater energy we truly are becomes so drastically diminished, so constrained, the cells begin to shrivel from lack of Life energy. The body is then reduced to bare survival conditions, ultimately dying from the relentless suffocation of its cells. But *only* the body dies, not the Life force you are.

In that state of suffocation, the poor cells, which must have a constant supply of Life force, are now compelled to respond differently to the negative vibrations seething throughout the body. Since their own well-being has been compromised through lack of that critical energy, they have no alternative but to allow dis-ease to take over. If disallowance of the Life force continues, the cells can no longer reproduce themselves. At that point, they cease their physical existence and simply recycle back into the pure positive energy of well-being from which they came. So do you.

We call it death, but the only thing that ceases to exist is your physical form, not You.

Scientists already know that the body can live far longer than it does now, like centuries. Yet these incredible instruments we take for granted aren't going to keep running without gas, so if someone is no longer excited about their life, and the energy stops flowing through them, what we call death is the result. But only to the body, not to You.

It's not the tainted smoke from the cigarettes that kills you; it's the disallowance of Life through the Life line. It's not the heart attack that kills you; it's the disallowance of Life that caused the attack in the first place. Let that Life force pour steadily and freely through you, unrestrained and unrestricted, and you could drink cyanide every day for breakfast without even getting the hiccups.

So isn't it interesting that the biggest fear we continue to vibrate, and then stuff away to vibrate even stronger, is the fear we have of death? Fearing death is a deplorable learned response we picked up long ago from a bunch of power-hungry fanatics, religious and otherwise, who wanted to play the game of "Let's Control the Masses." And they did, brilliantly. Get a bunch of people to fear something like death, and you've got them right where you want them—under your oppressive thumb.

That's how all the stupid rumors about devils and evil and hell and some big judge in the sky got started, by using fear as a mechanism of control. But since energy can't die, and all of us are most assuredly energy-based, fearing death is nothing but a monumental waste of time that evokes nothing but more negative energy. The sad thing is, we've been so cleverly taught to fear death, we've totally forgotten how to live.

However, if you do decide to change costumes, what happens is nothing more than a withdrawal from being physical, a disconnection from the body. The "You" that you are never quits. That part of you is forever and ever connected to eternal conscious awareness: You.

So what we erroneously call death is just a shift of focus, a bipping from one frequency to another. Will you ever be John Doe again? No, and would you want to be? But you don't cease to exist. You can't! You are the ongoing energy of Life scampering around down here right now on this particular playground. You are the pure positive energy of well-being, and *you can not kill energy!*

The importance of putting this fear to rest is no small thing, because even if we get all of our other Don't Wants switched to Wants, but then leave that one scary thorn in our side called death, we still have a fear vibration affecting everything, along with a mighty uphill climb to enjoyable health.

The easier way is to stop fearing this atrocious man-made myth and concentrate with everything we have on raising our frequencies to that Greater Part of ourselves which is the very essence of All That Is. Then we'd have all the heaven we could handle right here in our own little world, the way it was meant to be.

Everything Is a Cocreation

Many years ago, the mother of one of my closest friends was killed in a bizarre auto accident. As she and her husband were heading toward an underpass on the freeway, some swell kid tossed a boulder from the overhead crosswalk, sending it crashing through the window on the passenger side, killing Mrs. T. instantly.

Seems like one of those awful coincidences, doesn't it? Rotten luck. Bad roll of the dice. No, none of the above. It was a cocreation.

First of all, had either Mrs. T. or her husband been more plugged in to their Guidance, they would have taken another route, gone later, or skipped the ride altogether.

But secondly, and most important, this was not an instant happening of the moment. Like any accident, or illness, or calamity, it had been a long time cooking vibrationally. Mrs. T. had been operating with a closed valve for many years, smiling sweetly and chatting pleasantly while being deeply resentful of life's dealings. She was an exemplary victim who had been in strong resistance to the flow of well-being for a long, long time. And so was her young executioner.

Here's where we go back to the "Who's On First" routine. Whose vibration was responsible for the happening? Was it Mrs. T.'s, from her years of concealed pessimism? Or was it the kid's?

As it always is in any so-called accident, it was Mrs. T.'s vibration that did her in, even though it was a cocreation. She was pinging on a particular frequency and pulling in everything of like vibration which, in this case, wasn't too cool for her. Just simple physics; you hit that one tuning fork, and every other tuning fork on the same wavelength is going to respond.

Let's say on a scale of one to ten—ten being a wide open valve—Mrs. T.'s life of worry had caused her to emotionally vibrate at a destructive four for some time. On the other hand, the young lad had only a few years of feeling inferior to his peers, and grossly angry at life. Yet so strong were his feelings—and therefore his magnetic attraction—he too had reached that same destructive four.

Their courses were set. Sooner or later he was going to meet up with another four that was flavored with the same vibrations of unworthiness. For Mrs. T, if it hadn't been the rock, it would have been something else just as devastating from some other four.

Like a diver whose oxygen line has been severed, this frantic young man was simply lashing out in pain and anger from being cut off from his own Source of supply. In another way, so was Mrs. T. Finally, each in their own brand of pain, they were sucked into one another in a perfect example of cocreation. She had attracted her destiny; he had attracted his.

Someone or something need only match you in frequency, and the attraction begins. Which one (event, person, circumstance) will get to you first? The one with the strongest intensity. And you will keep on attracting and merging, attracting and merging, attracting and merging until you get so tired of the gloomy game, you eventually check out, as Mrs. T. did. Or you change your frequency.

If an accident involved two or more people, it was a joint exercise in negative attraction. If it was an accident that involved children too young to develop their own negative emotion, then those youngsters picked up their vibrations from their environment. If it was a plane crash, those on board of all ages magnetized themselves into the event.

Disaster, cataclysm, mishap, or disease: The brew of negative emotion that has perked over time to cause these happenings has come from an amalgamation of negative vortexes joining forces to form an electro-magnetic attraction so strong that ice forms on the wings of a plane to bring it down, or brakes fail in a bus to career it over a cliff, or a firestorm uproots what otherwise appears to be totally contented lives.

If we're living with our connection to that Life force cut off, sooner or later something's going to sock us, like a car, a flood, a train, or a tornado. (Ever wonder why a tornado will hit one house and leave the next? Now you know!)

If it's just a dent in your car, your valve has been partly open. If both you and your car got creamed, your valve has been pretty well closed. If you broke your leg on the slopes, your valve's been partly open. If you busted up your whole body, your valve's been pretty well closed.

I could go on, but it's sort of valve-closing to dwell on all this stuff. My point is that nothing, but nothing, but *nothing* comes to us by accident. Not our lotto winnings, not our new loves, not our illnesses, not a freak of nature, not an accident. They've all been drawn to us electromagnetically by our feelings and our vibrations. Nothing in our world ever has, or ever will, come to us except by our own vibrational invitation.

Now don't go flying off into Panicville if you've been a jaded basket case all your life. That's not an automatic ticket to cancer. Close, but not automatic! You have only to find your joy, and that open-valve vibration will instantly override years of gloom and doom. You might have a little fender-bender, but that's all it will be. No big deal. Or maybe you'll have a little cold. No big deal. Just small reminders that you still have some resistance to the frequency of well-being.

And so, who are the main attractors? We are, always! It's our feelings, our valve, our resistance. No one is doing it to us. If we're attracting negatively, it's because we're vibrating negatively, drawing some other thing or some other one into our space in the timeless dance of cocreation.

Our Wellness Switch

The bottom line to all of this is that we simply have no damn business being sick, being in accidents, getting old, or even dying for that matter, but as we routinely turn off our wellness switch to block our cells from their source of Life with negative emotion, something's bound to happen.

So you might want to watch how you're expressing yourself. If you're saying "I *want* to be well" but your dominant vibration is saying "Help, I *don't want* to be sick," which way are you attracting?

If you're sick and saying, "By God, I'm going to beat this thing, I'm going to win this battle," from that position of defensiveness, what are you focusing on?

No matter how many people love you, no matter how much you give to the poor, no matter how well you run your business, no matter how delightful and pleasant a person you truly are, if you have negative vibrations of any kind running, even in your manner of speech, you're going to attract some kind of bummer.

Now granted, the primary vibrations of mass consciousness are all around us, an endless exhaust of powerfully negative energy which we allow to govern us, knocking us about like a ship in a storm without its rudder, and usually making for a pretty rough ride. That does not have to be. You don't ever have to be a victim to mass consciousness, or to any one person's negative energy: not your doctor's, your family's, your friends', your lover's, or the groups around you.

Just state your Wants in every day, write (and then speak) new scripts about your body, your health, your looks, your life. And pretend. Get into the feeling place of what you're pretending, and become one who is so aggressively flowing your own energy and vibrating in the frequency of joy that you override all that you—or anyone else—might have been flowing before. Not only will your body joyously respond, but there will be no more accidents.

Is it easy? No, it is not the least bit easy to switch focus away from a roaring illness, or pain, or unwanted weight. But you can talk yourself down a little bit at a time. You can open that valve a little bit at a time and reverse your body's direction.

You are far greater than your body, so never doubt you can do this thing. Laugh more at everything and lighten up. There is only one thing you need do in order to have the body you desire; you have to find ways to be happy. A little at a time at first, until nothing else in your world matters, not your body, your family, your old doubts—only your focus on being happy. That, in the final analysis, is what health and well-being are all about.

your suit
of well-being

Washington is a state with a lot of trees, to put it mildly. There have to be more evergreens in that state than insects. While I am more a lover of deciduous trees and their seasonal change of clothes than I am evergreens, I had come to feel a strong attachment to the magnificent beings which graced my five acres.

When folks came over who had never been to my place, without fail their first comments were always about how wonderful the place felt and how exceptional the trees were. I had giants on my property that were unlike anything for miles around, with fascinating clumps of mixed species growing out of the same trunk. Even the few deciduous trees that blessed the place were awesome in their height and design.

But my special, special friends were a bunch of little guys just outside my fence, next to the road. All along Washington roadways are endless clusters of new little fellas doing their damndest to catch on and grow, and I had a fabulous long row of them. They grew fast, and by the time I had been there for three years or so, they were up far enough to create a sizable screen against traffic noises.

I loved them. I don't know why, really. Maybe it was their spunk, their steadfast determination to grow almost sideways out of the raised earth or to survive in the poorest of soil conditions. I don't know why, but I surely did adore them.

While I may have been following somewhat of a spiritual path in those early years in Washington, I was a long way from having my valve open. I blamed the weather for most of my moodiness. I was concerned about the remote location of my property. I missed my friends in California. And, though I was enjoying writing my first book, I was constantly focused on my lack of money, tipping the scales considerably more to negative vibrations than positive, and creating an open invitation to some form of disaster.

Then one day, one memorable summer's day I shall never forget, I heard the sounds of heavy equipment outside. I looked out my window to see a huge city weed cutter hacking down my street trees. I came unglued and dashed screaming to the street, but it was too late. The last of the beautiful trees I had watched grow from babies to six feet or more had just fallen. I don't ever remember howling in such anguish. They had just taken my beloved family, and I was devastated.

Over the next couple of summers, more yearlings caught on and grew. Try as I would not to become attached to them, I did. I was so proud of their guts, and just as amazed by their stubbornness. They weren't tall enough for the city to worry about yet, so I felt we were safe for a few years.

When the trees grew to be five- and six-footers, I knew we were getting close to chop-down time again. But now I was into the Law of Attraction and keeping an open valve to the best of my ability. There was very little fear in my world, no apprehension over safety, and a new-found love and appreciation for the wet and gooey-cold Washington weather. My vibrational scales had tipped well into the positive. I was happy, my valve was more open than closed, and I knew—I just knew— that my hardy young friends would be safe for as long as I lived there.

Sure enough, one summer's day I heard the heavy equipment truck again and went outside. There was no panic in me; I just went outside. The cutters had just finished slashing down a long row of my neighbor's roadside trees. Then they swerved out around mine to pass them by and started swacking at the property next door. I flagged down the driver and asked why he had skipped over my trees. "Oh, I dunno know, lady, they just seemed so pretty there, I thought you might want to keep 'em. You want me to take 'em down?"

So Safe, So Secure, So Happy

Our Expanded Self vibrates in a frequency we would call—if we could feel it—pure, unadulterated ecstasy (must be nice!). It would stand to reason, then, that the greater part of our being is operating in a frequency, or rate of vibration, a tad unknown to us at this time; what we would call *reeeeeeeeeally* happy. Since happiness and well-being are synonymous, that means there's a part of us—the biggest part—that knows nothing but unconditional, timeless well-being, for if you have one (high frequency joy), by the laws of physics you must have the other (well-being).

So here it is: When we're vibrating positively and feeling good, or buzzing, or appreciating; when we're plugged in, focused only on the joys of our Wants rather than the frustrations of our Don't Wants; when we're in a state of being that ranges anywhere from contentment to euphoria; when our valve is open and we are allowing our primary energy to flood through us...*there is not one blessed thing in this whole wide world that can harm us.* Nothing! Not in business, not in the home, not on the freeway, not in the body, and not to cherished trees on our grounds. Not one bad thing can happen, for when we are in that energy, we are living—and flowing—the energy of our own omnipotent Selves which knows only pure, untainted well-being, and doesn't know from diddley-squat about negative vibrations.

The only thing that greater part of us knows is inexplicable joy, power, chutzpah, frivolity, and infinite security, because infinite well-being is what It is! And...*AND*...that is what we, as its physical extension, really are. Pure, unending, well-being. All we have to do is give ourselves a chance to let it be so!

If I seem to be laboring the point, you're right, because we're talking "the good life" here. When we're plugged into that high-frequency energy, when we're out of fear-based and into happy-based, when we're not spewing out negative emotions of worry, bitterness, doubt or guilt, we've automatically plugged into the good life of well-being where nothing can ever harm us physically. That's right! *Nothing can ever harm us!!!* Not the local mugger, not our old car, not the drunken dork on the freeway, not even Mother Nature.

Earthquake? Sure, you might sustain damage to your home if there's been only a slight tilting of your scales toward the positive. But you'll be safe. If you're not, best check your valve (when you recover). You can always judge the degree of your connection to Source energy, and the openness of your valve, by the degree of destruction to your home, or body, or car, or job...whatever. Big robbery in the home? Big sickness? Big tornado destruction? Big closed valve!

And please, "closed valve" does not mean nasty or mean. Just because someone was killed in a hurricane or bomb blast in no way implies they were anything but warm, lovely people. It simply means they had unconsciously enveloped themselves in all the negative vibrations of mass consciousness that cause one's life to be so tough.

But when our valve is open, and our vibrational scales are tilted even a hair more to the positive than the negative, we literally place on ourselves a suit of divine armor. So when we're plugged in, turned on, and the high frequency juices are flowing freely, we can't even worry about being worried about whatever it was we were in the habit of worrying about, which of course, just served to attract more of what we were worried about in the first place.

When your valve is open, when you make a decision to be in joy with life *no matter what,* you automatically step into a suit of absolutely impregnable well-being in which nothing bad can ever happen to you. It is simply a vibrational impossibility for "bad" to happen to you in that high frequency.

But aside from the *big* awful things we ward off by living in our higher energies, there are all the neat *little* things that start to happen, like the by-passing of my precious trees.

For instance, if you have moles underground, they'll only come up where no one can see them, or not at all, but never in your front yard.

Squirrels will go after someone else's bird food, not yours.

Your house may have termites, but they'll soon move on.

Trees may fall on your neighbor's home from an over abundance of rain, but yours will stand firm.

Loose dogs may poop in your neighbor's yard, but not yours.

Your friends may be caught in the snowstorm, but you'll get home safely.

Your area may be targeted for mail theft, but your box won't be touched.

If you're low on gas a million miles from nowhere, someone will come to the rescue.

If the flu bug is walloping everybody, it won't touch you. And you'll *always* miss the plane that crashes.

All this—and ever so much more—from being wrapped in your own Feel Good energy, the frequency that guarantees our well-being.

Bad Stuff

Every time I speak to a group about flowing energy, questions about world affairs and all the awful stuff that's going on, or has gone on, always seem to surface. "How come so many starving people?" "What about Hitler?" "What about the Indians," etc., etc., etc.

I don't want to spend a lot of time dwelling on these things, because in a sense we've already talked about them. But let's take a quick look at some of the most common questions to see if we can reach a once-and-for-all understanding that from the beginning of time, every experience in every life has been attracted through individual and/or group energy flow.

And hey, I'm no cold-blooded sadist, suggesting in these next few paragraphs that it's possible to watch someone beating up on somebody and feel swell about it, any more than I'm saying a detached "Tut tut, too bad" to the atrocities happening around the world today.

All I'm saying here is this is how it comes about. Because whatever is happening always comes back to that same bottom line: when we feel good (or happy, or pleased, or enthusiastic, or loving) as an individual or as a group, we're inviting good experiences. When we feel bad (or bitter, or guilty, or resentful, or distressed) as an individual or as a group, we're inviting bad experiences. That's the way of it everywhere, with all of us.

Rape

One person is thinking fearfully about what they don't want. Somewhere else, another person is vibrating on the same negative frequency, but with hostility rather than fear. The second person thinks about what he believes will appease his rage and fill his emptiness. One person is vibrating fear; the other is vibrating inner fury. By their own matching frequencies, they become cocreators to an ugly event.

If you don't give your attention to the things you do not want, they cannot become a part of your experience, because they will not be included in your vibrations. You can only attract the rapist, murderer, or robber by thinking emotionally about being that victim, or—*or*— by vibrating with other negative emotions that just happen to match the attacker's frequency. Your every emotion creates the experiences of your life.

Prejudice

Needless to say, there are all kinds of prejudice: race, religion, color, sex, body weight, education, etc. Yet the one who is feeling prejudiced against is the most powerful in this cocreation, flowing out strong negative vibrations of persecution, of being disliked, wronged, or victimized.

Please note: I am not arguing the rightness or wrong-ness of any group's grievances. This is simply to say that it is the persistent attention to injustices which attract more of the same. Creation comes from feelings.

Young Kids

What about young kids being raped, or being born unwhole, or starving in Africa, or being killed in regional wars?

Sad to say, they have usually picked up the negative vibrations from their folks well before being born.

Those vibrations stay with them and grow in direct relation to the vibrations of the adults who are raising them until the youngsters are old enough to decide they no longer want unpleasant experiences in their lives. These children have become victims by default.

How do you help a little one starving half way around the world, or a little one at home who understands no words as yet? Hold them—either physically or in your thoughts—with soothing vibrations such as "Everything is really all right, it's going to pass, you are so loved, etc.," taking care not to assign blame to any one or any group, which only contributes more energy to the abuser (or the situation), as well as the abused.

The biggest problem comes to those who make it to adulthood and continue to vibrationally relive their snarly angers of growing up, e.g., the abuse of their parents, their environment, etc. Only by overriding those old patterned responses of hate and mistrust can a person have any hope of not repeating in adult years what was lived as a child. We get what we focus on. Focus on an ugly past, and that past is magnetized into the present and future.

Teens

Suicides, car accidents, pregnancies, drugs, guns. When teenagers are raised in negative energy (which rarely shows on the surface) and are taught only guardedness from birth, they operate primarily in a state of fearful vulnerability. Feeling out of control, they live by negative wanting as they search for ways to reconnect with the positive energy of Life. Drugs, sex, and other taboos are what they choose to fill the void they feel, born of a life lived with little or no connection to their Source energy.

The apparently blameless auto deaths which seem so prevalent today may or may not come from that disconnected vulnerability, but their cause is never accidental. The bubbly young homecoming queen, the popular star quarterback, the kids just along for the ride in the back seat. A life of hidden fears, pressures, and anxieties of some kind finally manifest to attract these cocreations of immeasurable grief.

The Economy

In bad times, people talk about it everywhere you go, and it's all bad, bad, bad. Yet even in good times we seem compelled to attack *something:* Prices are too high, corporations too greedy, jobs too specialized, the president's not playing with a full deck, the government is out to lunch and corrupt to the core.

Pointing to anything—*anything*—with that negative vibration of blame or "Ain't it awful, tsk, tsk" flows that very same energy to the subject of attention, making it bigger, stronger, and more dangerous than it was before you started bad-mouthing it.

If you're waiting for the economy, the government, or anything else to change before you can be happy, you might have a long wait. But neither do you have to join in the griping which not only adds to the already sizable problem, but shuts your valve down tight.

When you get involved in this kind of gloomy, negative party-talk, either take your conversation and focus off of what is and change the subject, or walk away. Then, when you're by yourself and you want to really make a difference, flow some Feel Good energy to the government the way you would like it to be, to the presidency the way you would like it to run, to the industrial giants the way you would like them to function.

We can not separate ourselves from consciousness flow. We can not say, "Well, it wasn't MY fault this happened." Oh yes it was! It was—and is—the fault of each and every one of us. We are a part of that consciousness flow, and our energy affects the whole as strongly as adding drops of red ink to a small glass of water; the change is clearly evident. *We are not separate from the whole!* Everything we think and feel has monumental impact on the overall vibration of mass consciousness.

So see and then feel things to be the way you'd like them to be. It would take only a few of us doing this on a regular basis to initiate desired changes. A noble goal, perhaps, but it beats making things any worse than they are by "ain't it awful"-ing the situations you want to change.

Global Conflicts, Gang Wars

Whenever you see a group of any kind expressing hate or outrage, you're seeing a group very cut off from their flow of well-being, and completely out of harmony with their Expanded Selves. Living in bitterness and anger is living with one whale of a lot of negative emotion and a valve that's closed tight.

When valves are open, no gang law, no government ultimatums can ever be strong enough to set anyone against his brother, even within the context of the age-old bitterness in the near East.

Moral Issues

Abortion, the butchery of dolphins, the rain forests, the ozone layer, animal rights, evangelistic thievery, mercy killings, endangered species, etc., etc. If you are giving your attention to it, seeing only the horror, feeling the transgressions, experiencing the alarm, and joining everyone else in the "ain't it awful" syndrome, you are adding to it, making it bigger.

If you want to change something, you've got to change the way you're thinking about it. That's all there is to it. The reason all these things are getting so out of hand is that the media focuses on them with a gargantuan hunger, and therefore, so do we.

"Oh dear!" "Oh my God, no!" "I don't believe it!" "How terrible!" "What will we do?" "How could they!?" "Frightful!" "Appalling!" And the more we get all riled up about it, the bigger it gets.

Being against something isn't going to make it better. In fact it's going to make it worse, because now you're including it in your vibration, flowing more "ain't it awful" out there to join with other thoughtforms vibrating at the same frequency.

If you still think that in order to be for something, you have to be against something else, change your thinking. Instead, see and feel whatever it is you're crusading for the way you want it to be. Talk about it in that way, write about it, role-play it, take your destructive focus with its powerfully destructive energy off what you perceive as a negative condition, and find ways to open your valve when you think about it. In other words, quit with the Don't Wants and focus on your Wants. The moment you do that, the moment you refuse to wallow with the rest of the world in their endless discontent, you will become one who will make a momentous difference by flowing the magnitude of your higher vibrations.

Mass Killings

All right, let's get down to it. Genocides, bloodbaths, holocausts, massacres: Call them what you will, humans have been clobbering humans since the beginning of time. Will it ever stop? No, not until we let go of our intrinsic feelings of persecution that we hang on to as if they were some noble family tradition.

If we truly want to stop these heinous events, we would be wise to remove our focus from the sordid happenings of the past and turn our attention to matters which open us to well-being rather than hate. It is that very energy, that loathing and bitter anger over bygone injustices, which helps to perpetuate the grim mass slaughters going on this day all over our planet. We get what we focus on.

The Law of Attraction doesn't pick and choose. What applies to an individual applies to a group, no matter the culture, the religion, the race, or the sect. Negative focus attracts negative events, to ourselves and to the planet. Like attracts like, and we attract as we vibrate, not as we decide.

Our Mirror, the Globe

It's not right versus wrong or good versus evil. It's closed valve versus open valve, connected versus disconnected, happy versus unhappy.

The meanest and greediest people in the world are those who really want to feel good, but don't know how. They're in a living hell with no idea how to get out, or even the awareness that they have that option. One thing is for sure; our hate against them—no matter what they may have done or are doing—is only going to make matters worse. For everybody.

But how can we go off and live happily ever after knowing that so many abhorrent activities are going on all over the world? How can we allow injustices to continue? How can we be happy when there is so much suffering? How can we turn our backs as if we didn't care?

This may smart a bit, but the answer is that we're all here to have the experiences necessary to learn our various lessons, whether we're playing the role of good guy or bad guy. An injustice of any kind is always—*always*—a lesson for both sides.

Somehow, some way, no matter what the devastation or loss may be to our brothers and sisters around the world, it's imperative we come to accept that ugly cocreations are happening everywhere for individuals to learn whatever is necessary for them to learn, all having to do with how they're flowing energy. As appalling as their circumstances may seem to us, if we join in their pain we are reinforcing that pain along with the circumstances that caused it, not to mention that we're setting ourselves up for some highly unpleasant stuff of our own.

You can be feeling how lousy it is that we allow people to starve, and just that closing of your valve could be setting you up for a car accident, while adding to their starvation.

You can be feeling how awful it is that we still have atomic testing in the world, and just that closing of your valve could be setting your body up for the flu.

You can be feeling horrified at one country's heartless treatment of another, and just that closing of your valve could be setting you up for a flat tire.

Instead, you could be seeing and *feeeeling* those starving people as the healthy, happy people you know they have the wherewithal to be, and just that opening of your valve might help your new job come quicker, while offering those you are wrapping in high frequencies some much needed paints and brushes. (We can never paint their canvas for them; we can only offer our energetic assistance.)

You could be seeing and *feeeeling* the planet as fully restored against atom bomb testings, and just that opening of your valve might help your crops flourish while helping to nourish the planet.

You could be seeing and *feeeeeling* those two countries enjoying a grand new rapport, and just that opening of your valve could improve your marriage while helping to create new international relations.

But of course it's fashionable to talk about what's wrong with everything instead of what's right, so we're more easily drawn into negative vibrations than positive, sliding unwittingly into the "ain't it awful" conversations

271

or starting them ourselves out of habit for lack of anything else better to say. Those vibrations, joined with countless others from all of humankind, eventually show themselves in worldly devastation and chaos. Yes, it's the amalgamation of all the little "ain't it awful" vibrations that causes wars, and riots, and terrorism, and anarchy. Those vibrations have come from you, and they have come from me.

We cannot hold ourselves above responsibility for what is happening around the world today, for the planet mirrors the predominant vibration in which it is encompassed. We cannot say the awfulness is simply the result of others' evil, or wrong-doing, or even ignorance. What is happening to our planet and to the peoples upon it has been caused by only one thing: the vibrations from our own thoughts and feelings. Everybody's! Not just the Hitlers, or the Custers, or the Husseins, or the Kahns (all of whom have been aberrations created by mass energy). Everybody's!

So rather than the "ain't it awful's," when we finally start saying to ourselves "Nothing is more important than my feeling good," we can begin to break those destructive negative talk patterns. Then, by God, we truly start to make a difference with what is happening around the world.

Take the rain forests, for example. Instead of agreeing with everybody about how dreadful the destruction is, and flowing more animosity towards those who are doing the chopping, which only brings about more chopping, love the beauty of the forests that remain. Flow your appreciation for the life they continue to nourish, for the oxygen they are still contributing to the planet, and stay out of the "ain't it awful" energy that will eat up our oxygen supply faster than thousands of tree-choppers ever could. If only a few of us will do this, the chopping will soon cease!

And then there's our growing lack of energy resources that everyone's so concerned about, and our dwindling water supplies, and lumber, and clean air, and heaven knows what else. Darn right we should be concerned, for we approach those things in the same way we do money. "Oh gosh, we're running out." "Oh gosh, there's not enough to go around." "Oh gosh, how will we get more when it's gone?"

So guess who's creating the shortages!? We are! It's that very concern we all have over not having enough that's diminishing our supplies. Each and every one of us is responsible for manufacturing those shortages, when in fact there's no lack of anything: jobs, forests, water, gold, or lovers. There can't be, for the universe does not operate on the principle of lack; lack is strictly a man-made phenomenon. When we start flowing appreciation to what's there, and feeling the enormous abundance of this perfectly balanced planet instead of focusing on her dwindling resources or the greed of plunderers, abundance of everything will return to create the heavenly playground we came here to experience.

If it's people you're concerned about, open your valve to the greatest love you can muster, and flow it out to those beings of your concern. See them in their states of perfection, rather than lack. See them happy and contented, no longer suffering from war, or pestilence, or famine. This will do more—more quickly—to assist those in need than all the plane loads of goods that always seem to go astray, for it will help these people out of the victim mode (if that is their deeper intent) toward their own first steps to attracting well-being. It will offer them paints and brushes. Once that vibrational invitation is offered, if a change is sincerely desired by all who are participating, it will happen. Then walls come down, countries make up, gangs diminish, terrorists evaporate, and wastelands prosper with food for all.

If it's the ailments of the planet that are your worry, see her in health, not disease. She's been drenched for so many eons in negative energy, this is hardly a time to add to it by talking about all the terrible things we're doing to her to make her worse. Talk about what's right with her, not what's wrong. Quit with the "ain't it awful" energy. Then dolphins multiply, forests grow, ozone layers mend, waters clear, oceans heal.

See your world and all who live upon her as abundant and well, and you will help her to get there.

See her in peace, and you will help to bring it about.

The only thing preventing our global desires from flourishing on this planet is the phenomenal mass force of perpetual negative vibrations which cut us all off from the primal Life force of well-being. That force of energy is so consummate, so absolute, if only a few of us will maintain this vision, backed with the vibrational joy of it being a reality, that supremely positive force will override the depressed vibrations of billions, and this planet will do an about-face...fast!

It's Everywhere: It's What You Are!

Actually, the majority of the world is quite well off. Just take a look at your coworkers, your neighbors, your school friends, your club associates. Most haven't been mugged on the streets recently. Most have acceptable jobs and homes. Most are sufficiently healthy, and if you look closely enough, you'll probably even find some who could be classified as moderately happy. It's the same in nearly every country in the world.

We have a glut of statistics to tell us otherwise, fearful figures of doom fed to us daily by our media to keep us nervously focused on—and tuned into—how horrible conditions are around the world:

"X-percent of world economies are collapsing."

"X-percent of the world population already has God-knows-what, and it's growing by X-percent monthly."

"X-percent of teens are having abortions and committing suicide."

"X-percent of kids have guns in school."

"X-percent of new diseases can't be cured."

"X-percent of purple-eyed males will lose their tans before marriage."

"Awful! Dreadful!"

Forget the damn statistics! They're simply a result of a bunch of us flowing fearful energy to what we're seeing and hearing. If you don't want to be another statistic, forget about them!!! As long as you're into Feel Good energy, no economy, nor bug, nor gun, nor flood, nor plane is going to down you. Not unless you send out the vibrational invitation.

There's just no getting away from it; the over-whelming balance of power on this planet is on the side of well-being *because that is the natural, omnipotent state of All That Is, including you and me!*

As ugly as it is, the suffering we see and hear about is an infinitesimal part of the whole of well-being, simply the magnetic results of some one or some group vibrationally disallowing the wellness that could be theirs if they only knew how to switch to the well-being channel.

The message is clear: Close our valve to anything, and we close it across the board. Close that valve of well-being to anything, from starving kids to vanishing species, and we shut out consummate well-being in every aspect of our lives.

Or close it off because you're tired of standing in line. Close it off because they delivered the wrong pizza. Or close it off because your ancestors lost their lives in the Holocaust. It doesn't matter! Closing it off is closing it off, automatically shutting out everything that comes with that higher energy, from abundance, to health, to uncommon happiness. Truly, is one stupid annoyance or some ancient lifelong resentment really worth such gargantuan privation?

In the midst of a divorce, or losing a loved one, or some tragedy to you or to others, you're going to feel bad, of course. But make a decision to feel bad for only a short time. Then say to yourself that's enough. It's time to flood you and anyone else affected by the events with love and appreciation. It's time to find things to feel good about and go on.

The moment you make that decision to change your energy, whether it be sadness from a divorce or anger over polluted lakes, the entire universe coalesces *in that instant* to cascade well-being into every crevice of your physical existence. It dumps it all over you, and around you, and through you. The only thing you have to do is say *YYYEEESSS!!!* to it all, and to Life, and wake up to how it good it feels to feel good.

Then you know from the very depths of your being that everything really is all right. No matter how it may look, no matter how it may seem, no matter what the media may report to the contrary, you and this precious planet, and most who are on it, will always be all right.

thirty days to breakthrough

Whenever I find a miraculous thirty day cure in a book I've purchased, I instantly toss it out. I am not an advocate of thirty day plans. In fact, I detest them, which is obviously why I designed one for myself within days of being introduced to the laws of deliberate creation.

Having said that, I have to tell you somewhat red-faced that while those incredible thirty days turned my life around by giving me proof that change was possible, the first ten days were a nightmare. In fact, working through those days was the hardest thing I had ever done from giving up drinking, to stopping smoking, to breaking up (which I was actually fairly good at).

But the results, of course, were startling or else I would not have continued. Never had it entered my head that it was possible to live life without some degree of concern, not to mention full-blown stress or outright panic. And yet that is precisely what was happening. I was learning to live without worry. It was astonishing. I seemed to have found a means to live in a state completely counter to what I believed to be normal.

While I live the four steps of deliberate creating almost every day now, if it hadn't been for that thirty day introductory program I designed for myself, I doubt I would have continued. My addiction to negative emotion was too ingrained, too much a way of life to give up in the blink of an eye. I would not have known where to start or how to proceed, no matter how great I thought these teachings to be.

Those first thirty days gave me such an enormous head start into learning how to take charge of and control my energy flow, that I've just about blasted every major fear I ever had—known and unknown—out of my life. Oh sure, I'm still a little skitzy about driving on icy roads, so I only do it when I'm sure I'm feeling okay. I still have some trouble speaking up for myself in intimate situations, so I only do it when I know my valve is open. Then it's a breeze. I sometimes lock my doors if that's going to make me feel better on down days, but genuine fear of break-ins is simply nonexistent.

And money? It's cascading in now with ease, and has been for quite some time, but I found out early on in my program that money would come in or stay away in direct proportion to my energy flow. If there had been no money coming in, I knew my valve had been closed with worry and fear. When money was more abundant, I knew my valve had opened some. When no money was coming in, I had to do a lot more of what I call "flip-switching," the rapid altering of one's energy from negative to positive. I had to find ways to get me out of whatever worry-habit I'd been in, and open up that valve. Then, as long as I kept my valve even a little more open than closed, money would come, but only in proportion to how much Feel Good energy I could muster.

Sure, I still focus negatively, but only for a brief time—a few moments, a couple of hours, sometimes even a day or two if I really want to feel like old times. But then I've had enough, and turn myself back around. I am simply no longer willing to sacrifice all my Wants and dreams and well-being for self-indulgent negative feelings over some stupid negative event. And I no longer charge in like the Lone Ranger against unwanted conditions to fix them, fix them, fix them. Indeed, old dogs most assuredly *can* learn new tricks.

But old dog, young dog, or somewhere in between, there is not one reason under the sun, not one excuse in this whole universe why you can't do this too, if you want to. A freedom of life is waiting for you that is beyond any capacity I have to describe, a freedom so unnaturally extraordinary that one can only know it through the joy of living it.

I'm talking about total personal freedom: freedom from boredom or monotony, from needing to prove or justify, from needing to need, from anxiety, and from all the imprisoning Shoulds of life we have so staunchly placed upon ourselves.

I'm talking about the freedom to exist as we desire, the freedom to acquire, to be outrageous, to prosper, and even to excel if that is a desire.

I'm talking about creating your own utopia, not next year, not in the next decade, but now.

That's where those first thirty days launched me. No, not all at once; this thing is on-going and will be for as long as I'm in this body. Some days are better than others, but *all* days hold more enduring joy than I ever thought possible, because I have the keys. Whether or not I use them is my choice, but one thing is for certain, I have no more excuses on which to fall back.

A mild warning, however. If you do decide to embark full tilt on this thirty day turn around, you could be facing a major battle with your fears. Old habits die hard, and your fears are not going to like it that you're thinking about cutting them loose. Frankly, neither are you. Yet all we're dealing with here is habits. That's all, just comfy old habits.

Our Need to Need

This relentless habit we have of negative thinking is so much a part of how we define "normal," most of us wouldn't know who we are without it. We'd lose our footing, for living in that vibration is the same as being hooked on drugs; once hooked, life can't go on without a fix.

I was speaking recently about the Law of Attraction and deliberate creating at a rather large Twelve Step gathering with folks in recovery, and found a fascinating dichotomy. On one hand there was eager acceptance of the principles, even a twinge of excitement. Yet on the other hand there was an obvious fear of letting go of the need to need.

One gal said, "I think what you're saying is exciting, but you've overlooked one thing: I need to keep coming to these meetings for my own growth. I need these people, or I'll go under again. I didn't have my valve open when I came six years ago, and it was these people who helped me get it open. If I leave now...well, I'd be afraid to do that. I'd be afraid to be out on my own like that."

Her valve was *not* open. This gal's addiction to fear had long ago turned into a need; her fear had become her fix. She felt her props would be knocked out from under her if anyone dared suggest she could wipe away her fears forever just by finding ways to feel better. To even broach the subject was sincerely terrifying to her. Fear was her identity, her security blanket, and she wasn't alone; that same reaction came from many. "Give me the keys to happiness, but don't you dare take away my insecurities or I'll feel stripped and vulnerable." Our ever-present need to need.

Then there's the unfortunate concept held by so many of us that before reliable recovery from any addiction or emotional disorder can take place, we must unearth all the painful junk we believe was dumped on us in early years. Another fellow said at that same meeting, "I don't see how you can feel better without regurgitating (his exact words!) all that horror we had to go through growing up." A habit of negative thinking turned into a need.

Our need for emotional pain to feel alive, or even for mild discomfort, is the greatest addiction ever known to mankind. Granted, we'll probably never stop having negative reactions, because contrast is what being physical is all about. But we most certainly can learn to allow the contrast, our likes and don't likes, without having to feel and flow so much negativity.

Three Frantic Months

But I hadn't learned any of this yet, so when interest rates went up and my prolific mortgage business all but vanished, I went totally ballistic. Loans dried up overnight, and overnight I went from positive to negative, blaming the condition—the rotten market—for my mood and state of mind. From "Man, this is hot!," I went to "Dear God in heaven, what do I do now?!"

With my focus glued to the declining market and my rapidly declining bank account, I anxiously cast a gaze to my upcoming infomercial that was almost ready to air. Surely this would pull me out of my financial mess. Surely this would save me. Surely there would be enough orders for this remarkable program to insure that the venture—and me—would thrive.

As had been true for most of my life, my addiction to problems once again became my security blanket. The only place I felt safe was wrapped in the familiar vibrations of negativity. I tried to turn on the buzz I had learned to play with, but was too fretful, and quickly gave up. Never once did I write a new script; I didn't know I could. All I did was lose sleep, drink too much coffee, yell at the dogs, and become more and more terrified over the vast sums of money I had spent, alongside of the sizable sums that were not coming in.

Then came the "what ifs?" What if the infomercial didn't work? What if I had spent the equivalent of five years' income and didn't receive enough orders to continue? How would I make a living again? How would I...what could I...what if...what if...what if...?

Once again I was creating a powerfully charged, very magnetic, and very negative vortex that was getting bigger by the second with each fearful thought I'd project. I kept trying to believe that things wouldn't have gone so smoothly for me the year before when I was making all that money while producing the program and show, if the success of the show wasn't "meant to be." Ha!

The half-hour commercial aired over an extended weekend in twenty different markets from Hawaii to New York and every place in between. I don't have to tell you what happened. There's not a Want in the universe that could have made it through the thick vibrations of my Don't Wants that were pleading, "I don't want this thing to fail; oh please, I don't want this thing to fail!" My valve was sealed, the door to my toy store was bolted tight, and my resistance to anything even remotely resembling well-being was larger than the Milky Way.

The size of the disaster sent me deeper than ever into fear. For three frantic months I ran around like a chicken with its head cut off in the Hi Ho Silver mode, my valve slammed shut, trying desperately to generate some income while maintaining a constant focus on a train of things unwanted. Never once did I let go of my unceasing blame of—and anxiety over—conditions. All of them! The market, the lack of savings, the lack of income, the TV disaster, the production bills still due. I did not like what I was looking at. Needless to say, the harder I looked, the more of it I got!

Finally, in answer to my anguished cries for help, I guess the universe took pity and slipped in some assistance on a sort of "take it or leave it" basis. Not big dollars (not any dollars), not new ideas, not even people to help—just some teachings. The principles of the Law of Attraction had been unceremoniously dumped in my lap.

Introduction to the Beginning

As excited as I was about these new teachings, to blithely jump into the four steps of the Law of Attraction would have been utterly impossible for me in the beginning. I was mired too deep in fear. With eighteen hours a day of ever-increasing anxiety, I was so awash in negative focus, negative feelings and negative vibrations that, without some kind of starter program, I knew I'd give up before I'd begun.

So I said to myself, "Okay, this shouldn't be too tough; I just have to find a way to stop thinking about things that get me uptight. No big deal. I'll just stop thinking about them for thirty days, then I can get on with the rest of the four steps."

Dreamer! It was a very big deal. But with a determination born of being on the bottom again and no where else to turn, I dove in and refused to give up.

If, indeed, you do desire to embark on the magnificent journey of becoming the deliberate creator you came here to be, I strongly urge that you dive into these thirty days too, before playing around with anything else. If you'll stay with it, the thirty days will identify the depth of your negative habit, giving you an invaluable bench mark from which to fly. At least it did for me for me. I had to establish where I was before I could chart a course. Man oh man, did I ever find out where I was.

So this was my start, my own eager—though thoroughly naive—beginning to shake loose the vibrational shackles in which I had been so unknowingly bound for decades. This is the thirty-day program I designed not a day after receiving the Law of Attraction material. I'll tell you straight from my journal how it worked for me and what you might expect along the way.

There are only two steps to my introductory program:

1) Remove your focus from *any major thing* that is currently causing serious fear (worry, concern, anxiety, stress, etc.), *AND KEEP IT OFF!*

Notice I didn't say to remove your focus from all things negative, just the current, pressing items, because these are easiest to spot and feel! They are always major, in-your-face Don't Wants of some kind that are causing you to be uptight.

If thinking about your empty bank account makes you tense, stop thinking about it *right now* and flip-switch to Number Two (see next page) right away. If thinking about your pending divorce generates that sinking feeling in the pit of your stomach, then stop thinking about it *right now* and flip-switch (see next page) as fast as you can. If thinking about your upcoming licensing exam is making you queasy, then stop thinking about it *right now* and flip-switch as fast as you can.

In my first thirty days, I personally didn't get into talking to myself or writing new scripts; that was far too complicated early on. However, if you do want to reassure yourself out loud or write a new script, go for it. Just remember that in these first thirty days it's vitally important to have a subject immediately available for you to flip into and quickly switch vibrations. That's the only way I found to begin breaking my insidious habit of "negative."

2) Establish a flip-switch topic for each day by finding one new item about *yourself* to appreciate.

A flip-switch topic is one you've established for the day. It's ready for you ahead of time to flip into the moment you realize you're feeling anxious, or a little down, or even moderately out of sorts. It's a topic you've chosen to have handy so you don't have to frantically search for some valve-opening thing to think about.

Don't think that finding something about yourself to appreciate is namby pamby. Believe me, it's tough. No matter what our position in life may be, most of us hold such great distaste in acknowledging our own attributes or talents that the thought of having to dig up a new one each day for thirty days can be really irksome. Happily, it's that very distaste which makes this exercise so valuable, for the process of digging up a new subject each day, along with the considerable effort it takes to stay focused on the thing, gets us so involved while we're stewing about it, we ultimately forget about the exterior worries.

So, what's to appreciate? Well, how about your hair, or your clean nails, or your singing voice, or your expertise with figures, or love of birds, or great body, or leadership capabilities, or acting talent, or strong hands, or finesse in parenting, or proficiency in skiing, or position in the company, or sales abilities?

If you think you can't find thirty things to appreciate about yourself, find them anyway. Then, when some habitual worry comes sneaking into your day, and you catch yourself in that hypnotic state of seemingly unbreakable focus on whatever it is you're worried about, you now have something waiting in the wings to immediately override it. You flip-switch *INSTANTLY* to your daily topic.

Now this is important: Stay with whatever topic of appreciation you've chosen for that day, no matter how absurd it might seem. In other words, don't bounce around with your daily subject of self-appreciation just because it makes you feel silly or you think you might like something better. With the ever-present help of your Guidance, you chose it for some reason, so that subject is yours for twenty four hours. Keep it!

Then, think about your daily appreciation item when you're *not* in fear. Think about it every minute you remember to do it. That kind of concentrated, high-vibrational focus will do more to break up your habitual worry vibration—fast—than you can imagine.

The First Ten Days

That's all there was to my program:

1) Keep my attention off anything that caused me to worry (which mostly pertained to finances), and

2) In its place, instantly install—flip-switch to—whatever was up for me that day to appreciate.

For the first three days, though, I hadn't developed the flip-switch process, and those days were incredibly rough. I was bowled over by the depth and duration of my negative attention spans. I found I slipped into worry at the blink of an eye. I was constantly uptight. No money was coming in and lot was going out. My ads weren't working and neither was the new salesperson I had grabbed in panic who was more into lack than I was. I tried to figure out what I wanted, but it all kept coming out in Don't Wants, so I gave up on that routine until I knew more about what I was doing.

It seemed as if this ever-present undertone of worry never left, even when I was smiling at people or talking cheerily on the phone. I'd hang up the phone and promptly wonder where the next loan was coming from, then realize what I was doing and try desperately to find something else—anything else—to think about. Since that didn't work, I was really floundering.

The hours went by slowly in those first three days. I was appalled at how many times in each hour I was focusing on my lack, a habit that was hard for me to fathom since just a few months before, the money had been pouring in like Niagara Falls. But I had the key now, and so help me, I was going to figure out how to use the fool thing.

By day three I was finding that probably 97 percent of my days were given over to worry, concern, anxiety, fear. That awareness depressed me thoroughly, then made me furious, which surely didn't help. I had no idea I had been worrying so routinely, so unknowingly. Talking to myself was useless, and writing a new script was impossible in my frame of mind. That's when I knew I had to find something ready-made to flip into, something with a nice easy focus, yet with a good high vibration. Thanks to my Guidance, I chose self-appreciation, thinking that would be fairly easy. Oh sure! Not only was it harder than I had anticipated, but I found the toughest part was staying there once I got there, which just made me more determined to continue.

At any rate, self-appreciation is what I chose, and instantly found that switching from negative to positive was much easier to do. Now I had something concrete to flip into, although I was finding it difficult to *feeeel* the appreciation, as opposed to simply thinking it...to *feeeel* it with an intensity that might start a buzz, even if the item for the day was nothing more than my shaved legs.

Sometimes I had to walk outside, take myself away from the office environment, and just stand under a tree until I could jump-start with an outer smile and get to that Gentle Inner Smile where I could finally overlay, with feeling, whatever item of appreciation was up for the day.

By day five I knew things were starting to turn around. Something was working—slowly, yes, but working. Although I could still only get into a really up-feeling place for a quarter of the day, the rest of the day would go fairly evenly without that incessant somber focus on lack.

During those first ten days, I didn't think I was going to make it. The more I had to flip-switch, the more depressed I became that this vibrant person (me) whom people had always viewed as being so positive, up, and happy, was nothing but a common, run-of-the-mill worry-wart, the very kind of person I used to tell people to stop being!

As the days wore on, I began to doubt I could ever reach that coveted time of actually getting through sixteen to eighteen hours without some degree of anxiety. Sometimes I would get so discouraged I'd scream at the universe, break into tears, and shove my hands in my pockets to go sulking outside for a walk in profuse self-pity.

Indeed, many times during those first ten days the possibility of learning to live without that familiar and even comforting vibration of concern that had been such an ally for the better part of my life seemed beyond all hope. What was causing me even more anguish was the distressing realization that I had this much fear to begin with.

Well, I had broken out of other addictions, and by damn, I'd break out of this one no matter what it took.

On day six (no, I'm not going through all thirty days), for no apparent reason, I went into a wildly deep depression and tears. I was feeling frustrated and angry but had no idea why. (I found out much later it was from a chemical change in my body.) Finally I went out and sat under one of my favorite trees for a while to help me calm down so I could flip-switch over to my daily appreciation. It took about forty-five minutes before I could plug in, but I did, and to my delight there were no more tacky feelings for the rest of the day.

Today if I get emotionally sideswiped like that, I instantly ask myself what Don't Want I'm focusing on or what's been bothering me, and usually find the answer quickly so I can talk it out, talk it down, and let it go. But back then, so early in the first inning, unless it was something obvious, I just tried to change the feeling.

As the first ten days began to wind down, I was aware of dramatic changes beginning to take place. Those out-of-nowhere sensations of foreboding that would wash over me for no apparent reason throughout the day were down to about two, from dozens. The overwhelming preponderance of negative vibrations had ceased, and with that realization I felt as if I had just conquered Mt. Everest nude. I was euphoric!

Also during those first ten days I became aware of how difficult it was for me to allow myself to fantasize, to want, to desire. Oh sure, I'd give vent to the usual things like more money, enjoying more time to do my work and so on, but rarely did I ever allow myself to indulge in my deepest dreams. If a fantasy did cross my mind, such as my lifelong desire for a secluded second home on a beautiful mountain lake, I'd simply sigh and shove it deeper inside to remain a forbidden longing.

I decided to nip that stupidity in the bud, and on day eight went out to split some wood, a particular passion of mine. I began scolding myself out loud (tough love) that darn it all, it was high time to bring that old hidden longing—and any others if I found them—out of the closet, turn it into a open-faced Want, and allow myself to feel the excitement of it, no matter what.

And I did. For one splendid hour, after turning on my buzz and stepping into some Feel Good, I chopped wood and talked to the dogs and me about my cabin in the woods by the lake. I described the smells, the trees, the dock, the cabin decor, the sparkles on the water at sunset. The hour flew by in seconds. I had broken through a barrier totally impregnable until now, the barrier of giving to self. I had allowed myself the joy of bathing in a fantasy and turning it into a Want. I had just turned another corner, and I knew it.

Sure enough, that week the synchronicity started. I saw "my lake" on TV the very next day. I found it on a calendar. I saw it in a magazine ad as if the universe was saying, "We heard you, kid, keep it coming and it's yours!" (As of this writing, it almost is!) Once again, I was euphoric.

By day nine, it was time to pay bills again, and I was uneasy. How would I feel? Could I stay out of fear of lack? Could I flip-switch my focus?

With a vise-like determination to pay attention to my feelings, I went to my desk. Thank heavens the monthly process was easier than usual, though I found it difficult to flip into—and maintain—a focus of appreciation. So I broke into song. Why not? Anything to crack that ancient habit of dreading the tenth of the month. It worked fairly well, but I ended up going out into my field to enjoy the late afternoon quiet and get my buzz going. There were no more negative feelings for the rest of the afternoon or evening. In my journal, that last sentence is underlined!

I knew I was on a roll. Ideas were starting to pop all over the place. I would deliberately try to push myself into a negative feeling *and found I could not do it!* But when one snuck in, I'd smile like a Cheshire cat, pat myself on the back for recognizing the feeling, and flip-switch vibrational gears.

Finally the day came, that long-awaited day, where I knew I had completely relaxed about income (though I still had none) to the point of being honestly unconcerned. God, what a fantastic feeling that was!

Out of years of habit, I found I'd still cut loose with all sorts of negative statements like, "No, sorry I can't go with you, I'm too low on funds and don't have enough coming in." Of course I'd feel glum the minute anything like that popped out of my mouth, but from there it didn't take much to find what had caused the feeling (always a Don't Want), and I'd flip-switch myself right out of it.

Day by tough day, I was watching a lifetime of unconscious negative thinking and negative emotion dissolve. I was breaking out of an addiction so deep, so profound, I never even knew I had it. There was no debate; changing my focus and my feelings was not only possible, it was happening. I waited impatiently to see the lucrative results, a really dim-witted thing to do!

From Ten to Thirty

The next twenty days were roller coasters. On the up and easy-buzzing days, I was showered with fantastic ideas to substantially increase my income. But the down days weren't just a little down, they were under the Grand Canyon with a strange new exaggerated moodiness. No one had told me—or any of us attempting to control our energies—about this rather unpleasant but apparently common occurrence that seems to happen when we start pulling more high-frequency energy into the body.

(We know now these swings come from the body acclimating itself to the prolonged periods of higher vibrations, which in turn cause a dramatic change in the body's chemical makeup. Since emotion—which is negative and physical, unlike feeling, which is positive and etherical—is chemically induced, the mood swings are simply chemical adjustments taking place. Some folks have experienced these mood swings rather profoundly, some only moderately, but everybody seems to have something to say about them. Fortunately, this passes. In fact, you can feel it letting up by about six weeks and usually gone altogether within three months.)

These rock-and-rollers would appear out of nowhere, smacking me in the gut when least expected. Frankly, there were days when it was so bad I simply said, "To hell with it" and didn't even try to jump-start my way out. By the next day or two, though, the black cloud would have passed, and I was back into my program full blast.

But no matter what mood was left over from the day before, there was one morning ritual I created, loved, and never missed. That was beginning each morning with a loving conversation with my Inner Being/Expanded Self. Down on my knees out of reverence to the Life I am (and to keep me bolted in one place while I did my thing), I'd outline my Wants for the day, week, and decade, pausing just long enough at each Want to allow its feeling tone to wash through me. They were reverent moments, humorous, and poignant, and I treasured them as part of my designed program. (I notice an emptiness and lack of direction whenever I let that ritual slide, which I sometimes do all too frequently.)

On up days, I could turn on a high in a heartbeat, slipping with ease into the feeling place of whatever appreciation I had chosen for the day. On days that didn't start out up, it took a little longer. But the most thrilling thing to me was that up or down, fear of any kind was clearly taking more and more of a back seat. The down days had no specific focus of Don't Wants or stress, just basic doldrums. There was a new spring to my step, a song in my heart and on my lips, an almost constant smile on my face, and a thrill of life and wonder of creation I hadn't experienced since...since I don't know when.

Although I had taught myself the year before to buzz without really knowing what I was doing, with the downward turn of the market I had retained so much negative focus on outside conditions that I had long since forgotten about buzzing. But I was revving it up again like an excited rookie at spring training.

I understood now that "turning it on" meant first getting my attention off Don't Wants. Whether I was flowing to actual Wants, or to my appreciation item for the day, or just for the fun of it, I knew I was at long last beginning to stop the flow of attraction by default. So I'd buzz, be in love (still one of my favorite up-feelings), be enchanted with life, and feel the energy of high joy tingling throughout my body.

By now I could flip-switch either into a particular Want or into my item of the day. If I found myself thinking about where the next loan was coming from, I'd instantly feel that soppy wet cloud around me, realize I was focusing on lack, and waltz myself right out of it. It was glorious.

And my kicky new game of watching for those wild synchronicities that start to happen once a Want gets launched was so entertaining, it was almost becoming an obsession. I would decide, in an up buzz, to find a new restaurant with special views, superb food, and charming waiters, and in a day or two a friend would call out of the proverbial blue with the suggestion of just such a place for us to visit!

I put a special kind of heavy white work shirt on my Want list that stores had apparently discontinued, and three weeks later I got a hit to go to an out-of-the-way discount store for some copy paper. Bingo! My shirt was hanging all by itself on display, *the only one in the store!*

Although I don't eat much meat, I had a craving one day for a juicy hamburger, got another hit to go to a new *hardware store* (?), and found a brand new market had just opened next door with the most deliciously fresh ground meat I had ever had! Over and over, obvious confirmations that living off higher frequencies was really working.

My monthly ratio that used to be 30/30 (thirty days out of thirty days with worry or anxiety) was now more like 17/0/13 (seventeen up, zero with actual fear or anxiety, and thirteen in that weird downer), a colossal improvement any way you looked at it.

But my eagerness to reap the rewards was dry-docking me. As I look back, I can see I was looking for results in the form of dollars as early as two weeks, a really stupid thing to do, since all that did was keep my focus on what wasn't there.

Finally, it was Day Thirty. Where was my overflowing bank account? Why wasn't my phone ringing off the hook for loans? Why was it taking so long to implement my new ideas? There I was once again, being disappointed over what *hadn't* happened. My continual "Where is it? Where is it?" was the same old negative focus just dressed up in a different costume.

Actually, money was indeed starting to come, albeit in dribs and drabs. I watched, fascinated. This strange, constant stream of a little here, a little there, obviously in direct proportion to my vibrational focus. At least with my valve somewhat more open than closed, I wasn't going backwards! My checking account was either staying the same (beats me how) or growing ever so slightly. Never again has it gone backwards!

It took a few months before I could allow the flood gates to open once again, but open they did. Not all at once, to be sure, but gradually. One Want after the other was finding its way to my door, some big ones, and lots of fun little ones.

And, without any help from me except deep appreciation for that terrific product I had somehow produced, *Life Course 101*—the audio-visual program I had created in accidental joy before ever knowing about the Law of Attraction—began to take off like gangbusters in different parts of the world.

I'd love to tell you that all my old habits were gone in thirty days, but of course that's not the case. Even today, with the money flowing in great abundance, it takes all my concentration to remember that what I accomplish is not about how hard I work, or how smart, but how I'm flowing my energy. So I keep writing new scripts, talking to myself constantly, and flip-switching.

Now, instead of an Appreciation-of-the-Day item, I have a Want-of-the-Month to fall back on which serves two purposes: it creates more vibrational time—therefore more passion—for the energy to flow to a specific desire, and it gives me that safety net of always having something ready and waiting in the wings to flow to when I need it the most.

In Training

Does it get easier? Good grief, yes. But if you're going to make a decision to take control of your life, have the things you want, do the things you want, be the person you want to be, and live the way you want with the people you want, there's something you might as well accept: you're in training for good!

You'll have up days, down days, fantastic days, cruddy days, deeply emotional days, and days when you'll be ready to throw in the towel. Yet I'd be willing to bet you won't, not now, not knowing what you know. Like it or not, it's doubtful you'll ever again be able to feel even a twinge of negative emotion without knowing you've just closed the door to all the things you ever wanted in life, be they material, physical, emotional, spiritual, or all of the above.

So yes, this is a life-long endeavor, and you're not going to learn it all in those first thirty days. You can break out of fear and worry in that first month, definitely. But then it's roll up your sleeves and plunge wholeheartedly into all the nuances of the Four Steps to Deliberate Creating, that is, if you want it all: prosperity, security, health, freedom, joy, aliveness, ingenuity, independence, fulfillment, your natural states of being, the way you were meant to be, the way you can be from here on in if you're willing to give it the effort it takes.

It's Your Play

This is nobody's show but yours, always has been, always will be. Nobody has ever held you by the ear lobes. Nobody has ever caused your life to be one way or the other. It's been your show from the outset, designed by how you were flowing energy, designed in every moment of every day by how you were feeling.

Now it boils down to what you want to do with the rest of your life and how willing you are to put forth the feeling effort to get it.

So here are some quickies, a fast rehash of the most salient points to bear in mind as you move into this exhilarating new world of deliberate creation. First, the main steps:

Step 1. Identify what you don't want

Step 2. Identify what you do want

Step 3. Find the feeling place of your Want

Step 4. Expect, listen, and allow the universe to deliver—and—(Step Four-A: *Keep your bloomin' focus off those blankity-blank conditions!*)

The Major Don'ts

- Don't take score too soon. If your Wants haven't started to appear yet, relax. And keep your valve open.

- Stop trying to fix anybody else; that's valve-closing stuff. You don't have to fix anything; you just have to stop thinking about it.

- Stop thinking the world has to change before you can be safe or happy. You create your own safety through your energy flow.

- Don't take anything that happens in your life for granted, good or bad, large or small. It came into your life because you magnetized it there, so pay attention to what you're creating.

- Stop focusing on, responding to, or worrying about how to control conditions that haven't changed yet. That's only getting you more of the same.

- Don't try to label how you feel when you're down. Stop calling it guilt or frustration or whatever. Just know you are out of sync and find a way to get back in.

- Stop being a wimpy wanter. Want big in quality, as well as quantity! And don't ever stop creating new Wants. The ultra high energy You are needs outlets to flow to. Create them!

- Stop thinking it can't happen. That vibration will guarantee it won't.

- Don't wait to feel good before you turn it on. Turn on all day long. Make it a habit. Buzz for no other reason than to keep your frequencies up, your valve open, and your resistance down to high-frequency energy.

- Don't take this all so seriously; that just makes for closed valves. Lighten up, have fun with this, and it will happen faster.

- Don't ever, ever, ever take uninspired action while your valve is closed, or while you're in the middle of a problem. Get your valve open first, then listen for your Guidance before acting.

- Don't try to find the ugly, dark, nasty causes of whatever it is you think is wrong with you. Stop it! All you're doing it giving more attention to what you don't want.

- Don't live for the end result, saying "I can't feel better until it happens."

- Don't beat up on yourself when you feel bad or close your valve. You only feel bad in a Don't Want, so congratulate yourself that you recognized it. Until you know what you don't want, how else will you know what you do want?

- Stop thinking about anything that closes your valve: any thing, any body, any situation, any event, any circumstance, any place, any movie, any food, any driver, any boss, any scene, no matter what, *NO MATTER WHAT!*

- Stop joining bandwagons of grievances loaded with closed-valve, disconnected beings. Flow your energy to what you do want, and affect the whole.

- Stop talking about your illness and causing your body to degenerate even more. Start talking about how your body is rejuvenating, and open your valve to allow it.

- Stop with the "issues" game. Having issues is nothing but an excuse to stay in negative vibrations.

- Don't yearn. It's just a negative awareness that you don't have something.

- Stop thinking that there's anything outside of you that is making—or can make—a difference.

- Don't be afraid to look at something you don't want. Look at it from all angles, then charge up your wanting, or your intending.

- Don't justify your feelings with a "I'm right and you're wrong," even though that may be the case. That closes your valve and plugs up the flow of higher energies to all other areas of your life. Remember, you plug up one, you plug up all.

- Don't regret anything; that's exceptionally heavy negative flow.

- Never, ever start a new project, business, venture, undertaking, activity, relationship, or *anything* before scripting it and flowing some excited, passionate energy to it *for a good long time.*

- Don't think it, feel it.

- Don't think your reactions, feel them.

- Get off your case. If you goof up, so what? Just decide to change it.

- Quit trying to find yourself. Begin, instead, to allow yourself. A grand life is your right. You *are* your life; therefore, you *are* your right.

- Don't ever forget, you are not Joe or Sally, you are not a carpenter or secretary, you are a force of Life. Act like it! Become it!

- Don't give up; don't you ever give up!

The Major Do's
- Allow yourself time in each day to dream, desire, imagine, intend, want, and time to flow energy to them all, flow energy to them all, flow energy to them all.

- Whenever you're feeling less than good, stop, regain your balance, and find a way to feel a little better, then a little better, then still a little better. Every Feel Better is a raise in vibration.

- Use everything you know to flip-switch out of negative focus into any kind of warm fuzzy.

- Make more statements in every day about what you want, and why: big things, little things, nonsensical things. The more Wants you have, and the more you get excited about them, the more dramatically your energy will flow.

- Make more decisions in every day, about your mood, your safety, your work, your relationships, your parking places, your shopping. As with Wants, decisions summon the energy and provide outlets.

- Ask yourself constantly, "How am I flowing my energy?" "How am I flowing my energy?"

- Give more time to your subject, and get off the fact that it hasn't happened yet. It's forming, it's happening, it's on its way. Believe it!

- Talk tenderly to yourself every day. Out loud.

- Watch for clues that things are happening, for concurrent events, for synchronicity.

- Keep writing outrageous new scripts.

- Pay attention to how you're feeling.

- Replace your "things to do" list with a "things to feel" list.

- Find new ways to feel a little better every day. Be creative. Be inventive. Be outrageous.

- Pat yourself on the back for every perceived obstacle you've created. Without them, you cannot know what you want.

- Think only about what you want, instead of the lack of it.

- Accept once and for all that you are the creator of your experience.

- Start your day with the intent to look for positive aspects about everything and everybody. Then intend to find them.

- Ignore how someone else is flowing their energy, and pay attention to your own, only your own.

- Remember that nothing—*nothing*—is more important than feeling good, even if it's just feeling better.

- Use your Want-of-the-Month like a life saver; it is.

- Start small to flip-switch from a negative to positive vibration. Soon that small thought will gain the momentum necessary to launch you into a major Feel Good.

- Expect your Wants. Expect them!

- Learn to turn on at will, no matter how you choose to do it. When you turn on, you open your valve, you lower your resistance, you vibrate positively, you attract positively.

- Stay alert to how you are *feeeeeling*, and the rest will be easy.

- Stay out of the past; it doesn't exist.

- Become aware of the feeling tones you roam around with all day long, from dawn to lights out. Stay awake. Become aware!

- Live in the feeling place of your Want every day.

- Or just live in Feel Good and watch how fast your Wants come.

- If you wake up feeling great, pump it. If you wake up feeling lousy, change it.

- Calm down, relax, soften up, get natural, be closer to You.

- Ferret out that beautiful sweetness deep within you. Find it, feel it, allow it, and fan it. Male or female, we all have it.

- Listen for your Guidance, and then act; never, never, never act before.

- Follow your impulses; that's your Guidance.

- Learn to look at contrast without having to cross the line into negative resistance.

- Practice flowing appreciation to street signs, brick buildings, red lights, or other outdoor objects as you're driving.

- Be aware of the very real obstacles you're creating with your resistance to your Source energy.

- If all else fails, smile a phony smile. Just cracking your face moves your vibrations up.

- If something's bugging you, get over it.

It's Your Ship

You can't screw this up. You can't make a mistake or a wrong decision. It's impossible. In fact, you never have made a mistake; you only invited lessons to help you get out of vibrating negatively. Now you know!

This whole business of creating our lives by flowing energies of a higher frequency than what we've been living is incredibly new for all of us. It's a gargantuan about-face, a momentous new orientation to life. So be gentle with yourself, take it easy, play with the energies, become curious, laugh more, smile more, experiment. See how long you can hold a buzz or how fast you can turn it on. Find out what gives you joy, then do it. Play with your Wants. Play with it all, but remember, this is all very, very new, so please, please, please don't get discouraged.

We're like toddlers on training wheels just learning to maneuver in our new world. Everything in that toddler says "get up and go." So it does, again, and again, and again, no matter how many times the tumbles may come. That's called passion...and practice.

Practice is what this new way of thinking and being is all about. It has to be; it's too new, too foreign. Right now, this concept is just so many words on paper that may sound enticing, but the proof is in the pudding. And that means practice!

Practice flowing the energy. Practice flowing it to your Wants, or practice just flowing it. Learn to turn it on at will...in any situation...wherever you are...whomever you're with...whatever's happening. You control your life by controlling your reactions to life. So practice!

After you get through with your thirty days, design your own new program to keep the interest jacked up. Maybe a week of feeling gratitude. Then maybe a week of feeling wonder about everything, or reverence, or awe, or excitement. Then maybe a week of feeling amusement, a week of being enthusiastic, a week of being in love, a week of feeling "God, it's good to be alive," no matter *what* is happening around you.

Practice in the odd-ball moments while you're sitting on the john, disciplining your children, doing your income tax, holding a board meeting, or working on the production line.

What's so new to us is grappling with this seemingly backwards concept that real Life is about feeling first and performing second. That's just utterly backwards to us. Only practice will bring the fruits of that outrageous new concept into being.

You can't think it; you gotta feel it! So practice becoming a lover. If it's something you want with a passion, love it all over the place. Caress it emotionally in the most tender, yet ardent vibrations. Embrace it with fervent devotion. Cradle it to your bosom. Enfold it with a depth of love so blazing, so afire, so beautiful it takes your breath away. Practice flowing passionate love. That's warm fuzzy-ing big time!

Yes, life may get bumpier for a time because you've increased your desire, so you've increased your magnetic energies. But with that desire comes genuine Life.

So learn to feel, feel, feel...good or bad...positive or negative. If a feeling ultimately opens the doors to the treasures of the universe, how bad can it be? If you want it enough, you'll learn to feel it.

Then learn to feel good, no matter what. This whole approach has to be conscious, deliberate. Knee-jerk responses have to go out the window. If you want to change the conditions of your life, you have to change your vibrations, so practice until you can change them in a blink. If you're not feeling warm fuzzies, you're either flat-lining or feeling tacky. Either way, you're sending out negative vibrations.

If you have a problem, talk it out to yourself for ten or fifteen minutes every day. Explore it out loud until you've found out what's troubling you and you've talked it down. Every time you do that, you permanently leave a little more resistance behind until finally you've dumped enough to allow your vibrations—and your experience!—to change.

Just remember, the way you think is the way you feel, and the way you feel is the way you vibrate, and the way you vibrate is the way you attract!

So if you want it, feel it, feel it, *feeeeel* it 'til it's a warm fuzzy. If you can feel it, you can have it. You can have anything you want if you can feel it first.

The world can be your oyster. You have only to give your attention to what's coming instead of what's not here. Once you are comfortable doing that, by the powers that be and the power you are, you will begin to live the life you came here to live. You will be fulfilling your reason for being.

It's all energy. That's all this world and universe is. You can either be its master or its victim. By learning to control the tenor and flow of your electromagnetic energy, you are learning to take control of your own destiny, steering your ship wherever you desire. When storms come, you know what created them and what to do. You are in absolute control, headed toward reaping the sumptuous rewards of a life that is—to the fullest extent of its possibilities—at long last being lived!

Appendix

Much of what is written in this book will test one's intellect and logic to the fullest extent. "Magnetize events? Nonsense!" "Prevent good times and create bad times? Get real!" For those who find themselves challenged in that regard, as I once was, you may find this fun energy-proving do-it-yourself kit a help.

Get two wire coat hangers and cut an "L" out of each one, about 12″ long for the main part, and about 5″ for the handle. Cut a plastic straw to go around the handle so that they'll swing easily, then once you have the straw in place, bend the bottom of the handle up to hold the straw in place. They'll swing without the straw, but not as freely.

Now you have a pair of what I call Woo-Woo Wands. Hold the wands loosely out in front of you as if you were pointing a gun. Keep them about chest high and about 10″ from your body. They flap all over the place at first, in response to your energy, so give them a few moments to settle down and stop wobbling. Once they've settled down, you're ready to play.

With your eyes straight ahead, recall with feeling some very unpleasant event from your past. Depending on the intensity of your emotion surrounding that event, the wands will either stay straight ahead (weak intensity), or will point inward, tip to tip. The wands are following the electromagnetic bands around your body which have contracted as a result of the negative frequency generated by your unpleasant thought and emotions.

Now make your frequencies turn positive by thinking about something incredibly wonderful, or loving, or joyous. Or focus on one of your children, or a pet, and literally flood them with love. The wands will now expand outward quite rapidly as your energy field expands in answer to your positive energy flow.

To demonstrate how energy follows thought, focus your attention on an object to your far left or right, and watch the wands follow your thought. Or begin focusing on your Expanded Self, your Guidance, and watch them spread apart in reaction to the enormous increase in energy such emotional thought creates.

The more you play with this, the more adept you'll become at feeling the vibrational shift that takes place within you as you change from one frequency to another.

Author Contact

If you would care to comment on this book, or, if you would like a complete description of Lynn's workshops and how to arrange for them, send your letters to:

Lynn Grabhorn
Box 244,
800 Sleater-Kinney Road S.E.
Lacey, Washington 98503 USA.

Qty.	Title	Price	Can. Price	Total
	Excuse Me, Your *LIFE* Is Waiting	**$18.95**	**$24.95**	
	Shipping and handling (add $3.00 for first book, $2.00 for each additional book)			
	Sales tax (WA residents only, add 8.6%)			
	Total enclosed			

Telephone Orders:
Call (800) 461-1931
Have your VISA or
MasterCard ready.

Fax Orders:
(425) 672-8597
Fill out order blank
and fax.

Postal Orders:
Hara Publishing
P.O. Box 19732
Seattle, WA 98109

PAYMENT: PLEASE CHECK ONE

☐ Check   ☐ VISA   ☐ MasterCard

888-509-0200

Expiration Date:_____/_____

Card # _____

Name on Card: _____

Name _____

Address _____

City_____State_____ Zip_____

Daytime Phone (_____) _____

Quantity discounts are available.
For more information, call (425) 776-3390.
Thank you for your order!
I understand that I may return any books for a full refund if not satisfied.